OCCASIONAL PAPER 173

The Baltic Countries
From Economic Stabilization to EU Accession

Julian Berengaut, Augusto Lopez-Claros, Françoise Le Gall, Dennis Jones, Richard Stern, Ann-Margret Westin, Effie Psalida, and Pietro Garibaldi

INTERNATIONAL MONETARY FUND
Washington DC
1998

Production: IMF Graphics Section
Figures: Sanaa Elaroussi
Typesetting: Julio R. Prego

Cataloging-in-Publication Data

The Baltic countries: from economic stabilization to EU accession / by
    Julian Berengaut . . . [et al.].—Washington, DC: International Monetary
Fund, 1998
        p.   cm. — (Occasional paper, ISSN 0251-6365 ; no. 173)
    Includes bibliographical references.
    ISBN 1-55775-738-0

    1. Baltic States — Economic Policy.   2. Baltic States — Economic con-
ditions 3. Fiscal policy — Baltic States.   4. Monetary policy — Baltic
States 5. Structural adjustment (Economic policy) — Baltic States.
6. Economic stabilization — Baltic States. 7. Foreign exchange — Baltic
States.   I. Berengaut, Julian, 1950. II. International Monetary Fund.
III. Series: Occasional paper (International Monetary Fund) ; no. 173.
HG243.B2 1998

Price: US$18.00
(US$15.00 to full-time faculty members and
students at universities and colleges)

Please send orders to:
International Monetary Fund, Publication Services
700 19th Street, N.W., Washington, D.C. 20431, U.S.A.
Tel.: (202) 623-7430   Telefax: (202) 623-7201
E-mail: publications@imf.org
Internet: http://www.imf.org

recycled paper

Contents

Tables

Figures

The following symbols have been used throughout this paper:

. . . to indicate that data are not available;

n.a. to indicate not applicable;

— to indicate that the figure is zero or less than half the final digit shown, or that the item does not exist;

– between years or months (e.g., 1994–95 or January–June) to indicate the years or months covered, including the beginning and ending years or months;

/ between years (e.g., 1994/95) to indicate a crop or fiscal (financial) year.

"Billion" means a thousand million.

Minor discrepancies between constituent figures and totals are due to rounding.

The term "country," as used in this paper, does not in all cases refer to a territorial entity that is a state as understood by international law and practice; the term also covers some territorial entities that are not states, but for which statistical data are maintained and provided internationally on a separate and independent basis.

Preface

This occasional paper provides an overview of economic developments and major policy challenges in the Baltic countries since 1994–95, focusing on the period 1995–97. During that time, the Baltic countries moved beyond the first stage of transition, which had emphasized financial stabilization and the revival of economic growth. In the second stage, the Baltic countries had to address policy challenges stemming from the choice of exchange rate regime, fiscal management, development and supervision of their financial systems, strengthening the private sector, and preparing their economies for integration with the European Union. The contributions to this paper relied in large part on the work that was undertaken by the staff of the Baltic Division of the European II Department in the context of discussions with the authorities on use of IMF resources and Article IV consultations.

The study was a collaborative project directed by Julian Berengaut with assistance from Augusto Lopez-Claros and Odd Per Brekk. Helpful suggestions were received from John Odling-Smee and Thomas Wolf. In addition, the authors are indebted to Constance Strayer and Lilian Immers for secretarial assistance and to Linda Galantin and Xiaofen Chen for research assistance. Juanita Roushdy of the External Relations Department edited the report and coordinated its production for publication.

The opinions expressed are solely those of the authors and do not necessarily reflect the opinions of the IMF staff, Executive Directors, or the authorities of the Baltic countries.

List of Abbreviations

BFTA	Baltic Free Trade Area
BIS	Bank for International Settlements
BRO	Baltics, Russia, and other countries of the former Soviet Union
CBA	Currency board arrangement
CIS	Commonwealth of Independent States
CIT	Corporate income tax
CMEA	Council for Mutual Economic Assistance
CPI	Consumer price index
EBRD	European Bank for Reconstruction and Development
EFF	Extended Fund Facility
EFTA	European Free Trade Association
EMS	European Monetary System
EMU	European Monetary Union
ERM	Exchange rate mechanism
EU	European Union
FDI	Foreign direct investment
GATT	General Agreements on Tariffs and Trade
GDP	Gross domestic product
IAS	International Accounting Standards
ICG	Intergovernmental Conference
IMF	International Monetary Fund
MIP	Multi-Annual Indicative Program
NDA	Net domestic assets
NTB	National Tax Board
OECD	Organization for Economic Cooperation and Development
PAYG	Pay-as-you-go
PIT	Personal income tax
SDR	Special drawing right
VAT	Value-added tax
WTO	World Trade Organization

I Introduction

Julian Berengaut

The process of adjustment and reforms in the Baltics deserves attention for three overarching reasons: (1) the extent and speed of transformation from the central plan and political repression to the market and democracy; from plummeting output and living standards and high inflation to high growth, low inflation, and rapidly rising real incomes; and from reliance on the central bank and bilateral and multilateral sources for financing to accessing domestic and international financial markets; (2) the policy challenges the countries have faced in choosing and maintaining exchange rate regimes; confronting weaknesses in the banking system; protecting public revenues while adjusting the pattern of expenditures; and resolving problems of interenterprise and energy arrears; and (3) an opportunity for a cross-country prospective based on similarities in size, starting positions, external shocks, and policy objectives, and differences in the choice of policies and their timing.

The linkage between the policy choices, their implementation, and the policy outcomes is the basic theme of the volume. Chapter II provides an overview of macroeconomic and structural adjustment policies mainly since 1994–95. By that time, financial stabilization had taken hold which allowed a critical mass of structural reforms to be put in place thereby creating the conditions for the revival of growth. Chapter III surveys issues regarding the choice of exchange rate regimes in the Baltic countries, including recent experience, current challenges, and medium-term policy options. Chapter IV covers three broad fiscal issues: the evolution of the budget processes into a rational tool for public resource management, revenue mobilization including the factors that explain the Baltic countries' success in preventing erosion of the tax-to-GDP ratio, and expenditure management and rationalization. Chapter V focuses on developments in the financial sector of the three countries, taking as a point of departure the banking crisis that occurred in Estonia (1992, 1994), Latvia (1995), and Lithuania (1995–96); it concentrates on the evolving structure of financial markets and the restructuring of the banking systems that subsequently took place. Chapter VI discusses private sector development in the Baltics, namely, problems in its measurement, recent trends, and the necessary conditions to foster it, and the policy agenda for removing remaining obstacles. Chapter VII examines the Baltic countries' relations with the European Union (EU), concentrating on pre-accession issues and the implications of membership in the EU for the three countries.

Rather than a comprehensive review of economic developments and policy issues in the Baltic countries, the volume represent a partial overview of those aspects that have stood out in the transition through 1997 as interesting challenges with potentially broader applicability. The selectivity of the papers is heightened by its methodological approach emphasizing the cross-country perspective rather then employing country-by-country descriptions; the cut-off point for describing developments is, in most cases, mid-1997.

II   Overview of Recent Macroeconomic and Structural Adjustment Policies

Julian Berengaut and Augusto Lopez-Claros

The Baltic countries were generally considered to be among the more developed of the economies of the Baltics, Russia, and other former Soviet Union countries (BRO), with a standard of living at the outset of the transition well above the average for the former Soviet republics. On regaining independence in 1991, the governments of the Baltic countries embarked upon comprehensive programs of economic and political reform involving a move away from central planning to reliance on the market and the establishment of a market-based legal framework and institutions for economic activity. In the early stages, the authorities gave priority to eliminating central plan distortions in the economy: the bulk of domestic prices were freed; external trade and the exchange system were liberalized; and the privatization of small and medium-sized enterprises was begun.

The conditions under which these reforms were introduced were hardly propitious. The very large contraction of output during the early part of the transition reflected a number of demand and supply shocks, including major adjustments in the relative prices of tradable goods (in particular energy imports from Russia), sharp reductions in demand in the Baltic countries' traditional export markets (the former Soviet republics), the impact of disruptions to trade and financial relations among members of the Council of Mutual Economic Assistance (CMEA), as well as the gradual elimination of subsidies associated with the introduction of a more transparent system of prices. At the same time, price liberalization, adjustments in administered prices, and the elimination of the monetary overhang contributed to a surge in inflation, which reached some 1,000 percent in December 1992, sharply eroding living standards. The external current account registered surpluses in the early independence years, reflecting weak domestic demand and the external financing constraint.

Since late 1994 and early 1995, the economies of the Baltic countries have entered upon a period of recovery from the shocks associated with the early part of the transition. Critical to the emergence of a more stable macroeconomic climate was the intro-duction of stable exchange rate regimes in all three countries (involving currency board arrangements in Estonia and Lithuania). It reduced inflationary expectations and provided a credible institutional underpinning to the authorities' anti-inflation policies, institutional development of key economic agencies, and the continuation of fairly liberal trade policies. In all countries, economic policies were supported by IMF adjustment programs that provided significant financing as well as technical assistance and policy advice. Recovery has not, by any means, been smooth and has at times been accompanied by setbacks, including banking crises in all three countries that undermined public confidence in the financial system and led to a temporary slowdown in banking reforms. Inflation, however, has continued to decelerate steadily in all countries, and output recovered, fueled in part by significant inflows of foreign direct investment. The current account has moved into growing deficits, but large capital inflows (except in the period surrounding the banking crises) have resulted in balance of payments surpluses and the maintenance of adequate levels of gross foreign exchange reserves. At times, the pace of structural reform has lagged behind the progress achieved in macroeconomic stabilization, but all governments have reaffirmed their commitment to completing the next phase of the structural reform agenda, in particular accelerating large-scale privatization, reforming the legal framework, and strengthening the regulatory environment, with the aim of enhancing growth prospects over the medium term.

Economic developments and policies in the Baltic countries during 1995–97 are reviewed below, with a look at some of the challenges facing governments in the period ahead. The years 1995–97 marked a vigorous recovery in output, notably in Estonia. Also, headway was made in a number of crucial areas to bolster growth prospects, and attempts were undertaken to move forward with reforms on the structural front; in Latvia and Lithuania, these developments took place against a background shaped by the aftereffects of banking crises.

Fiscal Policy

The Baltic countries have relied upon a prudent fiscal policy stance as a key component in a strategy aimed at establishing a foundation for macroeconomic stability. By and large, they have been able to achieve this without recourse to large-scale expenditure sequestration and the associated disruptions and distortions to resource allocation, and while continuing to maintain the essential functions of the state. The main factor that made it possible was avoiding the precipitous revenue decline observed in many other transition economies. This, in turn, reflected a number of mutually supporting policy measures, including the willingness of governments to raise taxes when warranted (e.g., excises, to bring them closer to European Union average levels), limited recourse to tax exemptions or their outright elimination, the introduction of a broad range of initiatives to improve tax administration (e.g., mandatory use of value-added tax (VAT) invoices), and the creation of a credible environment for tax collection through the application of penalties and fines. Moreover, all countries have implemented fiscal policies in the context of predictable budgetary procedures, involving a reasonably clear legal framework and with governments making concerted efforts to operate within the limits provided by the constitution and budget laws.[1] It is also thought that pegging the exchange rate (either via currency board arrangements or a straightforward peg) and the associated constraints on central bank credit to the government have provided additional incentives for fiscal discipline. In particular, the banking crises that erupted in each of the Baltics did not have an adverse impact on inflation, which continued to decelerate in their aftermath. By constraining the financing options available to the government, the "hard" currency policies imposed a hard budget constraint that effectively prevented the monetization of budgetary support to problem banks.

In Latvia and Lithuania, and more recently in Estonia, controls—both administrative and rules-based—on local government borrowing may also have played a restraining role. Yet another factor that may have facilitated fiscal adjustment during the early part of the transition is the fact that the Baltic countries were net contributors to the union budget.

With independence and the onset of fiscal reforms, a "windfall" emerged, equivalent to some 5 percentage points of GDP in 1991 in Latvia and Lithuania.[2]

Indirect taxes (VAT and excise taxes) account for a large share of total tax revenue, as does the social tax collected by the social insurance funds. Current spending dominates the expenditure side of the budget, of which wages and salaries and transfers to households are the most important components; investment spending has remained fairly low. All countries have made good progress in establishing the institutions needed for fiscal management in a market economy, such as a treasury system set up to manage central government operations, a public investment program, and a tax system increasingly centered on the needs of a market-based economy.

The governments in all three countries have increasingly begun to cast their fiscal policies in medium-term frameworks geared toward further lowering inflation, fostering stable financial markets, and faster output growth, all with the objective of gradual convergence to Western European standards of living. This approach is also consistent with the authorities' medium-term plan for exchange rate management, which envisages the maintenance of a pegged exchange rate, though not necessarily in the context of a currency board arrangement in the case of Lithuania. An outstanding issue is the need to maintain high levels of revenue mobilization over the medium term to fund growth-enhancing investment in infrastructure and environmental protection, finance pension reform, and, in some cases, accommodate certain rising pressures for social safety net expenditures. In this context, the agenda for tax reform, supported by continued progress in the reform of tax administration, would allow higher revenue yields for the major taxes without increases in existing rates.

Increased government saving is the principal policy tool available to increase gross domestic saving and to finance a higher rate of investment and growth. A cautious overall fiscal stance would also be an appropriate response to some possible risks that may arise in the medium term, which, to a greater or lesser extent, affect all the Baltics, including (1) contingent liabilities, such as domestic bank deposit guarantees; (2) potentially costly programs to compensate depositors for lost savings deposits in state banks in the early stages of transition, and for land and property restitution; (3) large one-off expenditures without agreed financing sources, such as the decommissioning of nuclear power stations, or

---

[1]This is reflected, for instance, in rigorous adherence to the timetables provided by the law for budget formulation. There are no instances in recent years of missed deadlines as regards the various stages of the preparation and approval of the budget, notwithstanding considerable political debate during the various stages of its formulation. In Estonia, the state budget (covering the central government plus the Social Insurance and Medical Insurance Funds) is legally constrained to be in balance (though a drawdown in deposits is classified as revenue).

[2]Estonia had already reduced its net transfers from earlier, higher levels to about 2 percent of GDP in 1989. See Tapio O. Saavalainen,"Stabilization in the Baltic Countries: Early Experience," *Road Maps of the Transition,* IMF Occasional Paper No. 127 (Washington: International Monetary Fund, 1995).

clean-ups of contaminated sites; and (4) uncertainties over projections of key variables, including the international economic environment.

Money and Banking

The Baltic countries have moved quickly to establish market-oriented banking systems. They have sought to strengthen money markets, and in the aftermath of banking crises in all three countries, to promote financial deepening and confidence in their banking systems.

Monetary Developments

Since the introduction of their national currencies in 1992–93, the central banks of the Baltic countries have pursued a restrained monetary policy aimed at supporting the exchange rate peg and safeguarding the external position. The range of monetary instruments at the disposal of central banks has differed depending on the institutional arrangements (currency board arrangements (Estonia and Lithuania) versus a conventional central bank (Latvia)). Even when available, monetary instruments have been used sparingly, and in practice, monetary developments have generally reflected balance of payments movements. The money market in all countries remains relatively underdeveloped, in part because of significant differences in the financial condition of individual banks, which acts to hamper normal interbank transactions and therefore the passthrough of monetary policy operations. Nonetheless, activity in the money markets has increased appreciably in the last two years (albeit from a small base), in particular in Estonia.

Financial deepening has proceeded unevenly in the Baltics. Factors that have tended to constrain the process have included banking crises in each of the three countries and the attendant lack of confidence in the banking system (as evidenced by high cash-deposit ratios), as well as weak institutional foundations for well-functioning credit markets (e.g., effective bankruptcy procedures, registry of land and other collateral, transparent regulatory frameworks). Factors that have tended to accelerate the process have included the strengthened financial position of banks that remained in operation after weak banks were closed down and the easy availability of foreign financing.

The financial system has developed most in depth and scope in Estonia, which experienced its banking crises earlier in the transition (see section below). Since 1992, deposits and credit as a percent of GDP have grown steadily, and interest rates have played an increasingly important role as price signals in the market. Financial deepening has unfolded more slowly in the other two Baltic countries, where recent monetary developments have been influenced by banking crises in 1995 (Latvia) and 1996 (Lithuania). Following the closure of several banks, broad money in both countries declined sharply in real terms, and domestic credit fell as well. The banking problems, sometimes in conjunction with fiscal slippages, contributed to a temporary, but very sharp, increase in interest rates. For instance, interest rates on treasury bills in Latvia increased from about 20 percent in March 1995 to a peak of about 40 percent in October 1995. More recently, there has been a resumption in financial deepening with the gradual restoration of confidence in the banking system and strong capital inflows.

Banking Sector

Banking sector crises emerged first in Estonia in late 1992 and early 1993, then in Latvia in 1995, and finally in Lithuania in late 1995 and early 1996. The early stages of each crisis involved government intervention in support of troubled private banks, a central bank moratorium on the operations of some of these banks to address serious capital inadequacy problems, and subsequent closure or liquidation of several large banks. These developments initially gave rise to rapid shifts in deposits within the banking system and created temporary liquidity problems for relatively solid banks that were accompanied by a sharp rise in interest rates and net outflows through the balance of payments.

With delays in some cases, the central banks acted on several fronts to deal with the banking problems, namely (1) implementation of tighter prudential standards;[3] (2) stepped-up monitoring of banks through on-site inspections; (3) the closure of banks that are not in compliance with prudential standards; and (4) progress in adopting international accounting standards.[4] The use of International Accounting Standards (IAS) (and of Basle methodology for calculating capital adequacy requirements) required the banking systems to make adjustments in several areas, including in the provision for loan losses, the valuation of interbank balances, and the revaluation of fixed assets. Large exposure rules have also been

---

[3]These requirements, which were aligned with international standards, included tighter limits on insider lending, credit concentration, and foreign exchange exposure, and an increased minimum capital requirement and capital adequacy ratio. Also, stricter rules for loan-loss provisioning have been introduced.

[4]In Lithuania, parliament amended the Civil Code to abolish the full deposit state guarantee for individuals with accounts in state-controlled banks, thereby providing these deposits with the same partial protection that applies to other banks under the deposit insurance law.

tightened and made consistent with EU standards, and the definition of "borrower" has been broadened to include related individuals and entities. The restructuring of the banks in which the government retains ownership interests has likewise moved forward, albeit at varying speeds, and has involved programs to cut costs and rationalize operations, including through closure of branches. Options for privatization of the state banks are under consideration in Latvia and Lithuania; the five major state banks in Estonia had been either liquidated or privatized by the end of 1995.

Overall, indications are that the authorities' efforts helped strengthen the banking systems. Bank capital has increased, and total bank assets are recovering, surpassing precrisis levels. Moreover, there has been a process of consolidation in the banking sectors in the Baltics involving mergers, liquidations, and significant retrenchment. As a result, the number of banks in operation has fallen, and the number of "problem banks" has declined markedly, almost all banks being in compliance with the minimum capital requirement and the capital adequacy ratio.

Trade

Consistent with the desire to give an early boost to the integration of their economies with the rest of the world, the governments in the Baltics were quick to dismantle the restrictive and inefficient trade regimes inherited from the Soviet Union. This entailed removing quantitative restrictions and phasing out export tariffs for the vast majority of goods. It also involved the elimination of protection for domestically produced goods through the establishment of low or zero-rated import tariffs. There are no import subsidies, and export licenses essentially fulfill a statistical purpose. There are also no export subsidies, and remaining export tariffs apply to a fairly narrowly defined set of goods. Estonia, in particular, maintains one of the most liberal trade regimes in the world. In Latvia and Lithuania, only certain agricultural products continue to be protected; governments there have encountered strong domestic opposition in attempting to reduce tariffs on these goods. All Baltic countries have free trade agreements with the European Free Trade Association (EFTA) members; and trade agreements with the EU. On April 1, 1996, a free trade agreement between all three Baltic countries came into force and was extended to trade in agricultural goods in early 1997 with the aim of eventually establishing a full customs union. All countries have applied for membership in the World Trade Organization (WTO) and expressed their intention of joining the EU. In late 1997, reflecting Estonia's significant progress in establishing the main elements of a modern market economy, it was chosen as part of the first wave of countries in Eastern and Central Europe to start membership negotiations with the EU.

Privatization

The Baltic countries have made important progress in recent years in privatizing state enterprises, especially small and medium-sized enterprises. The share of the private sector in GDP is estimated to have risen from some 5–10 percent in 1991 to about 65–75 percent by the time the first stage of privatization came to an end during 1995.

In Estonia, virtually all small enterprises, about 1,500 in number, were privatized by the end of 1994, and the bulk of large enterprises were sold by the end of 1996. Privatization was given an early boost by a government decision to privatize all small enterprises by selling them, mainly via auctions and open tenders, to the highest bidder for cash. After some delays, partly because of political opposition, medium to large enterprises were privatized as of late 1992 using the "tender" method, which aimed at selling enterprises as quickly as possible consistent with finding effective owners. Bids were awarded on the basis of price, business plan, investment, and employment guarantees—in short, to investors able to provide both capital and effective corporate governance. Finally, in the privatization process, the government favored strategic investors (domestic and foreign) over management and employees, a policy that encouraged foreign direct investment. Outsiders more often brought modern management and marketing skills as well as an enhanced capacity for capital investment.

Under a separate program in Lithuania a large share of apartments and houses were also privatized early in the transition. In Estonia and Latvia, residential housing privatization has moved more slowly owing to administrative rigidities and problems encountered with restitution issues; for instance, in Estonia, the government is committed to compensate, either via restitution or with vouchers, all pre-1940 property. The fact that rents remain artificially low is also thought to have been a factor.

In Latvia and Lithuania, the privatization of small enterprises moved ahead fairly rapidly, but that of medium to large enterprises has proceeded slowly during the past few years. Many of the initial offerings did not generate sufficient interest, owing in part to the low participation offered and the poor financial condition of some of the enterprises put on the market.[5] Gradually, packages of shares in a num-

---

[5]In Lithuania, the process of valuation of enterprises on the privatization lists also took longer than anticipated, in part because of inadequate local administrative capacity.

ber of enterprises were auctioned increasingly successfully, and both the size of the interest sold and the relative attractiveness of the enterprises offered increased. Nevertheless, the delays meant that only about ½ of 1 percent of large enterprises in Latvia had been privatized by the end of 1997, and about 30 percent of medium- and large-scale enterprises in Lithuania had been transferred into private hands as of mid-1996.

In the next phase of privatization, Estonia has initiated plans to privatize the remaining large enterprises, which are mostly in energy, telecommunications, and transport. As for Latvia, the authorities have taken steps to accelerate the process, including opening nearly all sectors to foreign participation in privatization. And in Lithuania early in 1997, the new government widened the range of enterprises eligible for privatization by announcing the sale during 1997–98, via international tender, of a number of large enterprises in the transport, energy, and telecommunications sectors, as well as other enterprises in shipbuilding, maintenance, and air transport. The government also decided to abolish negative lists (which had been adopted by parliament in late 1994 to prevent the privatization of some 250 enterprises), including the majority of the enterprises in the energy and transport sectors.

The restructuring of privatized enterprises has been left to buyers, mostly on the basis of business plans submitted at the time of bidding. One factor that is thought to have facilitated a more rapid restructuring of the enterprise sector in Estonia is the presence of an effective Bankruptcy Law since 1992, which made it possible to initiate bankruptcy procedures against several hundred enterprises by the end of 1996. In conjunction with the drying up of budgetary subsidies to state enterprises from the outset of the transition, the Bankruptcy Law had a strong signaling effect vis-à-vis the enterprise sector. In sharp contrast, in Lithuania, not more than six enterprises were declared bankrupt during the period 1992–96, and a revised Bankruptcy Law was approved only in early 1997.

Notwithstanding the significant progress made, a number of challenges in privatization remain. Among them, land reform is perhaps the single most important obstacle to completing the transition to a market economy. While there have been some differences across the Baltic countries, slow progress in land reform has reflected governments' attempts to accommodate several competing interests simultaneously, in particular the rights of original owners, as well as complex procedures for the transfer and titling of land. The passage of land reform acts early in the transition established the right to private ownership, but at times, preemptive claims on land were granted to the original owners in the form of restitu-

tion. To further complicate matters, restitution of the land actually owned by original owners was not made mandatory; compensation in the form of privatization vouchers or comparable land elsewhere was to be possible if either the original owner preferred one of these two options or if the use of the land had materially changed (e.g., by the erection of a factory). Thus, unsettled restitution claims have rendered uncertain the final disposition of a substantial number of land plots. Even where pending restitution cases are not an obstacle, complex and costly procedures for surveying, titling, and securing local government approval for land sales (including questions of zoning and town planning) have also contributed to a slow pace of privatization. Moreover, in many cases, local authorities have responsibility for steps in the process for which they have neither expertise, financial resources, nor motivation to complete. Land reform laws have been amended, including simplifying survey procedures and establishing incentives for municipalities to privatize land (as in Estonia in April 1996), in an effort to overcome some of these problems. Progress will continue to be slow, mainly because the process itself involves the creation of a complex institutional and legal framework. For example, in Lithuania, parliament still needs to approve a constitutional amendment to allow legal entities to own agricultural land. More generally, the extension of land ownership rights to legal entities in the Baltic countries for both agricultural and nonagricultural land should do much to enhance the functioning of land markets and contribute to the development of collateralized mortgage lending. It would also bring the legal framework for the agricultural sector closer to that in EU partners.

Energy Sector

The problems of the energy sector in the Baltics have been closely linked to the large changes in relative producer prices of imported oil and gas in 1992; the difficulties of consumers in accommodating sizable price adjustments for goods with inelastic demand; and the need to return the largely state-owned companies in the sector to profitable operations in advance of privatization, while disengaging the government from tariff policy. Reform of the energy sector in recent years has been driven by three principal objectives: (1) to commercialize the operations of energy companies within a newly created regulatory framework that tries to balance consumer interests against companies' rate of return, and which also allows for price increases to cost-recovery levels; (2) to strengthen payments discipline for energy and energy products, particularly in respect of public consumption, thereby underpinning the commercialization of producers; and (3) to eliminate budgetary subsidies for energy, replacing them with targeted support for low-income consumers, as necessary. Considerable progress has taken place in most areas of energy reform, although significant delays have been encountered in commercialization of companies and the reduction of overdue bills.

A strengthening of the institutional environment for pricing policy has been a key ingredient in reform of the energy sector. This has involved the introduction of regulatory bodies with broad latitude to propose price increases for electricity and heating in line with a methodology for cost-recovery pricing. Although the recommendations are not always binding, it is anticipated that the threat of legal action against the energy companies will effectively make the recommendations a price ceiling and prevent the reintroduction of cross subsidies from residential to industrial consumers. In agriculture, the regulatory bodies have thus far sought to eliminate preferential pricing of electricity, and for heating, they have proposed raising the overall price level and abolishing preferential pricing for industrial consumers.

To varying degrees, the authorities in the Baltics have had to address the issue of nonpayment of energy bills. This problem has generally led to a cascading of overdue bills, including on external payments for energy inputs. For instance, in Lithuania, nonpayment of electricity bills (where billing did not necessarily reflect cost recovery) led first to arrears from the Lithuanian Power Company (LPC) to Lithuanian Gas and then to delays in payments to the two foreign gas companies and to erratic supplies. Moreover, energy companies in Latvia and Lithuania accumulated large tax arrears, with overdue consumer bills amounting to as much as several percentage points of GDP in 1995–96. In addition, the energy companies were often the largest debtors to the budget, and, in turn, the budget built up delays on payments for its own energy consumption. The authorities in these two countries took several measures in 1996–97 to deal with delinquent customers, notably increased use of cutoffs and improved budgeting in public organizations, which reduced the arrears stock considerably. Also, the 1997 budget in Lithuania explicitly included expenditure allocations (of ¼ of 1 percent of GDP) to clear energy arrears of budgetary organizations and established a netting mechanism to use state transfers to municipalities for direct payment of overdue energy bills. Fines were introduced for the heads of budgetary organizations with unpaid debts in excess of 30 billing days. Together, these measures contributed to a sharp reduction in the stock of unpaid bills during 1997. In Estonia, by contrast, the stock of energy arrears has been quite small, partly as a result of the approach taken by the government, namely, to foster open

competition among oil companies, to encourage energy companies to devise systematic and transparent billing and collecting methods, and to depoliticize the process for imposing financial discipline on energy users.

The move to increase energy tariffs to cost recovery levels throughout the Baltics has removed the need for further budgetary subsidies (traditionally paid as producer subsidies). However, as a social safety net measure, governments have introduced payments to consumers when combined electricity and heating bills exceeded a certain percentage of gross income. Governments have also accepted liabilities in respect of past arrears on unpaid production subsidies.

Agriculture

With Estonia leading the way, agricultural policy in the Baltic countries has gone through several phases during the last few years, the broad thrust of which has been to introduce a greater measure of flexibility and market orientation in the sector. With the exception of a limited number of export restrictions initially retained in Latvia and Lithuania to slow down price adjustments on the domestic market, most controls on agricultural marketing were abolished early in the transition. Support prices and subsidies were also eliminated early on in all countries, and during the following years, major agricultural products received no substantial price support. During 1993, state trade monopolies were abolished, and most remaining quantitative import and export restrictions were eliminated or replaced with tariffs and export taxes, with tariffs drifting upward over time, except in Estonia where they essentially remained at zero. In response to a cumulative decline in agricultural output of 40 percent over the period 1991–94 in Lithuania, some support mechanisms were reintroduced in early 1995 for the main agricultural products. More recently, tariff increases in Latvia and Lithuania have been partly reversed and most agricultural export taxes have been eliminated.

The liberalization of the agricultural sector in Lithuania, and to a lesser extent in Latvia, was given a boost in 1997 through policies designed to (1) reduce distortions in the commodity and credit markets; (2) increase targeting and transparency in the allocation of budget resources for agricultural support; and (3) reduce in real terms the claims made by the sector on budgetary resources. The linchpin of the reforms consists of changes to domestic support policies introduced in the context of the creation of rural support funds. Furthermore, the extension of the Baltic Free Trade Area (BFTA) to agricultural products was ratified by parliaments in 1996 and came into force on January 1, 1997. The agreement provides for complete free trade in agricultural and food products of domestic origin and is expected to stimulate competition in the countries' food industry. And in Lithuania, protection of domestically produced food was reduced considerably on January 1, 1997 with the increase in the VAT rate on domestic food production from 9 to 18 percent, the level applied to imported food.

Governance

All Baltic countries have taken initiatives in recent years to improve the legal climate for economic activity and to create a foundation for better governance. New chapters have been introduced in the penal code to deal with a variety of activities for which the legal framework was seen as inadequate, and new institutions within the government apparatus have been created to strengthen the capacity for the prosecution of economic crimes. Centralized data banks that can be accessed by different government agencies are being developed, and the experiences of other countries in dealing with economic crimes in general are being studied (e.g., tax evasion in major industrial countries, money laundering in various international banking centers). Progress has been particularly noteworthy in the area of institutional development, where over a dozen different government agencies in all three countries (e.g., the Ministry of Finance, Customs, the State Tax Service, the Prosecutor's Office) are actively cooperating in the identification and prosecution of economic crimes. Sometimes with donor assistance, customs offices are being computerized and border controls tightened. Laws on money laundering have been approved, and attempts are under way to strengthen the administrative capacities of key institutions to facilitate enforcement.

Among other initiatives that are expected to contribute to an improved climate for economic activity, governments have approved resolutions that call upon government officials (including those at the highest political levels) to publicly declare their assets. In Estonia, the authorities are presently considering plans to establish the office of an ombudsman and introduce an ethics code for the civil service. The former would help secure individual rights, while the latter would improve public knowledge of the rights and obligations of public officials. Lithuania has established a high level interagency Working Group to take the lead role in promoting the government's anticorruption efforts. The tasks of the Working Group are to (1) propose new legislation or amendments to existing legislation and, more generally, to introduce initiatives intended to support the government's efforts to create an environment characterized by the rule of law; (2) draft a Civil Service Ethics Code, the aim of which is to establish statutes for the conduct and exercise of civil servants' official duties and responsibilities; and (3) carry out a comprehensive review of all economic legislation (e.g., legislation on free economic zones, laws adopted in the context of the 1995–96 banking crisis) and examine its consistency with recent changes to the penal code and other decisions taken to deal with economic crimes.

III Exchange Rate Regimes in the Baltic Countries

Augusto Lopez-Claros and Pietro Garibaldi

The conduct of macroeconomic policy in Estonia and Lithuania in recent years has taken place in the context of currency board arrangements (CBAs). Under the arrangements (introduced in Estonia in June 1992 and in Lithuania in April 1994), the monetary authorities have virtually no discretion in conducting monetary policy since, under a CBA, the monetary base rises or falls in response to the central banks' sales and purchases of foreign exchange at the fixed exchange rate. Indeed, a currency board can be defined as an "arrangement that legislates a particular monetary rule," under which a country gives up all monetary sovereignty and allows changes in the monetary base to be determined entirely by the international balance of payments.[1] In Latvia, the currency has been pegged to the SDR since February 1994 and the conduct of monetary policy has since been overwhelmingly geared toward maintaining the exchange rate peg. Although the Bank of Latvia does have a range of monetary policy instruments at its disposal (e.g., reserve requirements, open market operations, a refinance facility for overnight loans to commercial banks, repurchase auctions, and auctions of central bank deposits), in practice, limited use has been made of such instruments and developments in the monetary aggregates have reflected, as in Estonia and Lithuania, mainly movements in the balance of payments and, to a much smaller extent, the extension of central bank credit to government. Thus, except for some institutional differences, all three countries have operated for the last several years in the context of a fixed exchange rate regime.

While there appears to be a broad consensus that the above approach to exchange rate management, supported, for the most part, by appropriately tight fiscal policies and structural reforms, has served the Baltic countries well during the first stage of the transition, a number of questions have recently arisen concerning its medium-term suitability. For example, how sustainable is a fixed exchange rate policy in the context of countries that, notwithstand-ing the significant gains made on the stabilization front, have rates of inflation that are still substantially higher than those prevailing in the countries whose currencies serve as the anchor for domestic inflation? What are some of the possible disadvantages and costs associated with the continued implementation of these policies and at which point and under what conditions should alternative approaches be considered? While much has been written on the introduction of currency boards, there has been comparatively less debate on the policy issues and choices confronting policymakers as they contemplate the costs and benefits of a move toward more flexible arrangements. In any event, even if a consensus were to emerge that no policy changes are warranted in the short run, alternative policy regimes should be kept under review (e.g., an exit strategy). Also, it would be important to examine contingency measures that might be required if the CBA came under pressure and to consider ways to strengthen "lender-of-last-resort" mechanisms.

Recent Experience

There has been ample discussion in the literature on the macroeconomic advantages of CBAs. These mainly stem from the liberal exchange system implied by the full convertibility of the domestic currency, which is guaranteed by the 100 percent reserve cover; fiscal discipline, which is imposed by the inability of the central bank to provide credit to the government (which forces it either to balance the budget or to seek alternative sources of financing, domestically or abroad); the payments adjustment mechanism to various shocks, which is implicit in the arrangement;[2] and, more generally, the transparency that is associated with the underlying institutional arrangements. These advantages are expected to engender confidence in the monetary

---

[1]Williamson (1995), p. 1.

[2]That is, the response of the money supply and interest rates to a balance of payments deficit that, through its effects on absorption, eventually brings about a reversal of the deficit. This process might turn out to be quite traumatic if the banking system is fragile.

system and thus create the conditions that foster investment, trade, and growth.[3]

To a greater or lesser degree all of these features have been present in the three Baltic states. At the same time, in all three, the available evidence points to an improvement in the effectiveness and credibility of the authorities' anti-inflation policies associated with the presence of the CBA or peg, as witnessed by declining inflation and interest rates under the conditions of output recovery and a strengthening of the balance of payments (Table 3.1).

In Estonia, the influence of the CBA on the government's stabilization policies has been well documented in a number of papers (e.g., Citrin and Lahiri, 1995). Estonia entered a phase of economic recovery in the second half of 1994, and output growth in 1995–97 has been led by the rapid growth of export volumes and strong domestic demand. Buoyant investment has reflected large inflows of foreign direct investment, sometimes amounting to some 5–9 percentage points of annual GDP. These inflows, in combination with a highly skilled labor force, have facilitated the transfer of technology, the renewal of the capital stock, and have contributed to productivity growth in the tradable goods sector.[4] There is a broad consensus that the CBA has made an important contribution to the effectiveness and credibility of policies, as reflected in the favorable macroeconomic indicators: cumulative GDP growth in 1995–97 is estimated to be about 20 percent; short-term lending rates, which stood at 40 percent at the beginning of 1993, fell to some 14 percent in 1997, and annual end-of-period inflation stood at 12½ percent for December 1997, compared with 42 percent at the end of 1994.

In Lithuania, the period of operation of the CBA coincided with a sharp decline in nominal interest rates. Inflation has likewise been on a downward trend; with the end-of-period rate in December of 1997 reaching 8½ percent, the lowest level since the outset of the transition. The country's overall external position has improved in the context of a more open trade regime and a reorientation of trade toward hard currency markets. Foreign investment inflows

remaining modest until 1996 (but recovered sharply in 1997) principally reflected delays in structural reform (notably cash privatization) and the more gradual emergence (for instance, in comparison with Estonia) of a favorable legal and regulatory environment with respect to foreign participation in domestic economic activity. As regards output, GDP growth has picked up considerably with cumulative growth in the period 1995–97 estimated at 14 percent.

A similar assessment can be made for Latvia where a strong perception has been created among economic agents that the exchange rate peg is at the center of the authorities' anti-inflation objectives. Since the peg was first introduced, foreign reserves have increased and been maintained at levels providing adequate import coverage; domestic interest rates, with some temporary interruptions,[5] have been on a downward path of convergence to international levels; and domestic monetary assets have grown, reflecting the higher level of reserves but without additional pressures on prices as the increase in money was associated with higher money demand. As in Estonia and Lithuania, inflation has also decelerated and output has entered a period of recovery, supported by some pickup in foreign investment and other capital inflows.

Evaluating the contribution of the exchange rate regime to an external outcome involves the counterfactual problem. Furthermore, the presence of other factors, largely exogenous to the exchange rate regime, is likely to have had an influence on the evolution of the above indicators. A case can also be made that the introduction of new exchange rate regimes in all countries had been preceded by a period of commitment to stabilization and reform (indeed, the perception of the existence of such commitment was an important consideration behind establishing such regimes) and, thus, some of the ex post improvement noted above may have reflected the beneficial effects of such policies. Other favorable elements linked more to the overall macroeconomic climate (and geographical location) than to the nature of the exchange rate regime per se, for instance, the increased availability of foreign financing, are also likely to have played a role. Nevertheless, the weight of evidence suggests that the CBAs in Estonia and Lithuania and the peg in Latvia (coupled with a strong independent central bank) significantly enhanced the credibility of the authorities' disinflation policies, often against a background of structural weaknesses and constraints (e.g., energy sector financing difficulties in Lithuania in 1994/95,

---

[3]For an overview of the issues see Williamson (1995). See also Baliño (1997). In a brief survey of the challenges facing central banks Fischer (1996, p. 37) observes that "the monetary theory of the currency board is exactly that of the gold standard. Provided the arrangement is credible, it brings the benefit of rapid convergence toward international inflation and interest rates . . . . there should be no mistaking the severe demands a currency board puts on monetary policy." This may partly help explain the relative infrequency with which monetary authorities have opted for CBAs.

[4]Estimates prepared by the Bank of Estonia suggest that average labor productivity in the tradables sector in Estonia increased by some 40 percent between the first quarter of 1993 and the second quarter of 1996.

[5]For example, in 1995 in the aftermath of the collapse of the largest bank, which resulted in some capital outflows and a contraction in the money supply.

Table 3.1. Selected Economic Indicators

	1992	1993	1994	1995	1996	1997
	(Percentage changes from previous period)					
Inflation[1]						
Estonia	942.2	35.7	41.6	28.8	15.0	12.5
Latvia	958.7	34.9	26.3	23.1	13.1	7.0
Lithuania	1,162.5	188.8	45.0	35.5	13.1	8.4
Real GDP growth						
Estonia	−21.6	−8.2	−1.8	4.3	4.0	10.8
Latvia	−35.2	−16.1	2.1	0.3	3.3	6.5
Lithuania	−21.3	−16.2	−9.8	3.3	4.7	5.7
Fiscal balance[2]						
Estonia	−0.3	−0.6	1.3	−1.2	−1.5	2.0
Latvia	−0.8	0.6	−4.0	−3.3	−1.3	1.3
Lithuania	0.5	−5.3	−4.8	−4.5	−4.5	−1.8
General government revenue[2]						
Estonia	34.6	38.5	41.3	39.9	39.0	38.9
Latvia	28.2	36.4	36.5	35.5	36.8	39.9
Lithuania	32.0	30.2	32.6	32.3	29.6	32.7
General government expenditure[2,3]						
Estonia	34.8	39.1	40.1	41.2	40.6	37.0
Latvia	28.2	35.3	38.2	38.2	38.0	38.2
Lithuania	30.2	35.4	37.4	36.8	34.1	34.7
Broad money						
Estonia	...	52.9	29.6	31.3	36.8	40.3
Latvia	...	84.0	49.0	2.7	19.9	38.6
Lithuania	...	100.2	63.0	29.0	−3.5	34.1
Interest rates[4]						
Estonia	...	30.4	25.2	16.3	13.8	14.0
Latvia	...	67.0	49.0	34.0	23.0	12.8
Lithuania	...	91.4	33.0	26.2	14.8	12.2
External current account[2]						
Estonia	3.4	1.4	−7.4	−5.1	−9.7	−12.9
Latvia	...	14.5	−0.2	−3.4	−4.1	−6.9
Lithuania[8]	...	−3.2	−2.2	−10.2	−9.1	−10.3
Real merchandise exports						
Estonia	...	38.7	26.5	22.4	−8.3	14.2
Latvia	...	...	−28.9	6.8	8.9	13.4
Lithuania[8,9]	...	...	0.2	33.3	26.1	22.8
Real merchandise imports						
Estonia	...	44.8	53.1	32.8	10.8	12.0
Latvia	...	...	18.9	23.6	22.7	13.1
Lithuania[8,9]	...	...	2.4	52.4	26.6	23.9
External debt[2,5]						
Estonia	3.6	8.3	7.3	6.7	6.9	5.6
Latvia	...	10.4	9.9	9.1	8.1	7.3
Lithuania	...	13.2	11.4	13.7	21.3	26.6
Debt service[6]						
Estonia	1.1	1.4	0.4	0.5	0.9	1.6
Latvia	...	1.0	4.8	2.4	4.4	7.4
Lithuania	...	1.5	1.3	2.5	3.3	5.3
Foreign direct investment[2]						
Estonia	7.6	9.1	9.1	5.6	2.5	2.8
Latvia	...	2.3	4.2	5.2	7.0	7.2
Lithuania	...	1.1	0.7	1.2	1.9	3.4
Gross official reserves[7]						
Estonia	4.3	4.9	3.2	2.7	2.7	2.8
Latvia	...	4.8	4.7	3.0	3.1	3.0
Lithuania	...	2.0	2.7	2.5	2.0	2.1

[1]End of period.
[2]In percent of GDP.
[3]Including net lending.
[4]Lending rates, in percent.
[5]Includes public, publicly guaranteed, and private debt.
[6]In percent of exports of goods and nonfactor services. Public and publicly guaranteed debt only.
[7]In months' of imports of goods and nonfactor services.
[8]Data prior to 1996 are not comparable.
[9]U.S. dollar value, official data, f.o.b. basis.

banking crises in Estonia in 1992–94, in Latvia in 1995, and in Lithuania in 1995/96).

Limitations and Constraints

While an exchange rate regime which reduces discretion can be operationally useful and enhance policy credibility, it can also impose constraints and potential costs that need to be kept under close review. This section examines some of the main disadvantages.

Risks of Overvaluation

A potential problem with fixed exchange regimes is the risk of overvaluing the exchange rate that may result if the arrangement is introduced while inflation is still relatively high, even if the level of the exchange rate initially chosen implied substantial undervaluation. The danger is not so much that inflation will not eventually be brought down to international levels but rather that the transition to these lower levels may be long and ultimately result in an overvalued exchange rate. Or, alternatively, that the inability to allow a nominal appreciation of the exchange rate will make it more difficult to contribute to a more rapid convergence of domestic prices to international levels.

The level of the initial peg that was chosen when the fixed exchange rate regimes were introduced in the Baltic states was heavily determined by the need to make the arrangements credible even at the cost of disequilibrium in the goods market implied by an undervalued real exchange rate. It was expected that this disequilibrium would work itself out over time, although there was practically no basis for projecting how speedily the process would be completed.[6]

The length of the transition period is obviously not independent of public perceptions of the government's determination to adhere to the fixed rate. A perceived weakening of such determination involving, for instance, a loosening of the stance of fiscal policies, is likely to lead to economic agents (wage and price setters) starting to build in premiums on wages and prices, reduce the demand for domestic currency, bid up domestic interest rates, and so on,

against possible future changes in the exchange rate, a process which is likely to slow down the process of convergence to permanently lower inflation.[7]

Relative price adjustments in the transition from central planning to a market economy are a key factor that has contributed to the persistence of higher inflation in the Baltic countries. The prices of previously heavily subsidized goods and services (e.g., food, fuel, housing, health care, among others) with a large weight in the consumer price index have all increased sharply, and such increases have not been offset by decreases in the prices of other goods, leading to upward adjustments in the price level. A measure of the extent to which this process of convergence in the structure of relative prices to that prevailing in the rest of the world was expected to continue following the introduction of the CBA or peg is provided, for instance, by estimates that suggest that consumer prices in 1994 in Latvia and Lithuania stood at levels equivalent to 30–35 percent of 1994 prices in Sweden and Austria.[8]

The risks of overvaluation have been mitigated in the Baltic countries by gains in productivity that have allowed the maintenance of an adequate degree of competitiveness during the transition, including the process of relative price adjustment. The potential for additional gains in productivity in the Baltic countries is thought to be large as the modernization of these economies continues and as they partake of the traditional benefits of greater foreign participation in domestic economic activity (e.g., nondebt capital inflows, transfer of technology and know-how, and so on) and a more open trade regime.[9] In general, there is legitimate concern that a domestic rate of inflation that is persistently higher than the rate prevailing abroad can eventually erode whatever "headroom" might have existed at the outset of the introduction of the fixed rate regime.

While there are some country-specific nuances, on the whole, there is no evidence that the evolution of the real exchange rate (measured by the usual consumer price–based indices) during the last few years

---

[6]While references are made in the literature to a consensus suggesting relatively slow adjustment speeds to real exchange rate disturbances, the issues are not settled, particularly since the extent of initial disequilibria observed for the Baltic states falls far from what has been observed in other cases. The particular consensus that is mentioned implies that disequilibria damp out at an annual rate of 15 percent, implying that it would take about four years to dissipate one half of the initial discrepancy between domestic and international prices (Rogoff, 1996). See also Parsley and Wei (1996) and Engel and Rogers (1996).

[7]An interesting variant of this could be seen in Lithuania in late October 1996 when, following parliamentary elections, uncertainty about the future direction of policies led to a swift and negative market reaction. One aspect of the private sector's response to this heightening of policy uncertainty was to accelerate efforts in the banking system to denominate loan contracts in dollars. See Baliño (1996), p. 20.

[8]For a more detailed discussion see Richards and Tersman (1995), Berengaut (1996), Lorie (1996), and van der Mensbrugghe (1996), where evidence is presented that suggests strong positive correlation between annual inflation and the size of the gap between domestic prices and prices abroad.

[9]Foreign direct investment per capita in Baltic countries still lags behind Central European economies in transition.

has been associated with a deterioration of their external position.

In Estonia, as in Latvia and Lithuania, dollar wages remain well below levels in Western European trade partner countries, and these relatively low labor costs are often cited as an important contributing factor for the growth of foreign direct investment. Export growth has remained buoyant in all three countries, and while the current accounts deficits have widened, especially in Estonia, international reserves remain adequate.

In addition, all three countries have remained largely free of indexation mechanisms and are perceived to have fairly flexible labor markets that have helped maintain competitiveness. There are no strong employer organizations and trade unions, and the governments have on the whole not intervened in the wage-setting process, with wage settlements generally based on firm-specific productivity developments. Levels of unemployment compensation are relatively low, while eligibility periods for drawing benefits are short. Furthermore, privatization processes have generally eschewed the use of restrictions on the employment levels and production profiles of privatized entities.

A recent updating of the trade weights used in the computation of the real effective exchange rate in Lithuania (which gives a somewhat larger weight to trade with the East and uses a more representative set of trade partners—e.g., inclusion of trade with Estonia and Latvia) shows a real effective appreciation between April 1994 (i.e., introduction of the CBA) and December 1996 of 15 percent (Figure 3.1). In Latvia, the real effective rate based on the consumer price index (CPI) appreciated by 12½ percent between February 1994 (i.e., pegging to the SDR) and December 1996.[10] With the CBA in place for a much longer period, the real appreciation in Estonia has been more pronounced—46 percent between January 1993 and December 1996; however, even this real appreciation is less pronounced if the calculation uses unit labor costs and export unit values or a tradable goods price index. Between the first quarter of 1993 and the second quarter of 1996 the real appre-

---

[10]The estimate combines a real depreciation against the currencies of the Baltic countries, Russia, and other countries of the former Soviet Union, which account for roughly 50 percent of total trade, and an appreciation with respect to the European Union (EU), which accounts for the rest; to the extent that a growing share of trade is with the EU, the relatively small 6 percent real appreciation may overstate somewhat Latvia's strong competitive position.

Figure 3.1 Real Effective Exchange Rates
(November 1993 = 100)

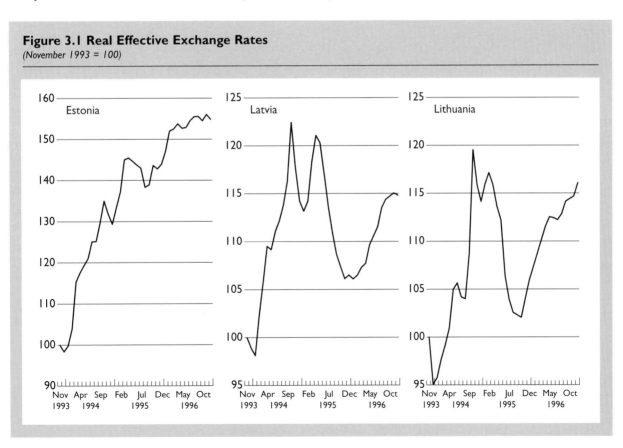

ciation is estimated to have ranged between 15 percent and 30 percent.[11]

Loss of Autonomy

Partly related to the difficulties that a country might face in adjusting to shocks, the constraints imposed by a CBA on the traditional functions of a central bank and the implementation of an active monetary policy can, in certain circumstances, have tangible costs. There may be instances when the presence of a CBA prevents an adaptation of monetary policy warranted by specific domestic conditions.[12] The loss of autonomy can be seen as an important potential disadvantage, particularly in the case of countries perceived to be in the early phase of the transition to a market economy, thus still subject to various imbalances and structural rigidities (e.g., distortions in the financial system, difficulties in collecting tax revenues). The extent to which this loss of autonomy is to be regarded as a problem is partly a function of the role that the authorities see monetary policy playing in influencing real economic variables (e.g., high unemployment, weak output growth). If the *primary* aim of monetary policy is to achieve sustained price stability (leaving to structural and fiscal policies the task of dealing with rigidities and supply constraints), then the relevant question is whether it is easier to control inflation with an "independent" monetary policy in the context of a flexible exchange rate or through some type of fixing, either through a CBA or some targeting mechanism involving little or no autonomy.[13]

In general, the scope for an effective independent monetary policy will be greater if (1) the authorities do not yield to the temptation of accelerating money growth in the hope of temporarily stimulating output; (2) money demand and supply functions are reasonably stable and predictable; and (3) monetary policy is not held captive to pressures stemming from the need to finance large fiscal deficits or large wage increases, or both. Whether these conditions will be satisfied in the Baltic countries in the period ahead is an open question. Financial policies have been on the whole cautious but some of this caution may have been itself strengthened by the CBA's proscription of lending to government or, in Latvia, by a policy that has put defense of the exchange rate peg at the center of the authorities' macroeconomic policies and that has been supported by a favorable track record of fiscal discipline. The economic transition itself (including policy instability), together with ongoing processes of financial innovation, is likely to create sufficient "noise" to make money demand functions relatively unstable, at least in relation to the instability confronted by policymakers in other countries further along the transition path. The exceptionally low money-to-GDP ratios in these countries suggest the need for gradual monetization over the medium term; such a process is akin to a structural change in the money demand function, which would imply high instability in the underlying parameters.[14] While unstable parameters are dealt with on a daily basis by central banks all over the world, the Baltic countries have to face additionally the disadvantageous combination of large systemic changes and scarce central bank expertise.

By the same token, for inflation control in the context of fixing to work it is necessary that the rate of inflation of the anchor currency be lower and more stable than the domestic rate of inflation and that the authorities' commitment to the fixed exchange rate be fully credible. The first condition is clearly fulfilled in the Baltic countries. The issue of credibility is more complex but there seems to be consensus that the CBAs in Estonia and Lithuania and the peg in Latvia have indeed enhanced the credibility of government anti-inflation policies. By doing so, they may also have helped minimize the output costs associated with disinflation. Further elaboration on the medium-term exchange rate policy options in the Baltics is presented in Section IV.

Lender of Last Resort

The constraint that in a CBA the money supply can grow only in direct relation to inflows of foreign

---

[11]The usual methodological and conceptual issues underlying a proper interpretation of such indices in the Baltic countries remain valid. While providing useful signals, about underlying cost, developments, and price competitiveness, the indices need to be interpreted with caution and in the context of a more systematic analysis of other developments in the balance of payments.

[12]Williamson (1995) gives the example of Hong Kong in the early 1990s when the link to the U.S. dollar involved importation of low interest rates from the United States at a time when a domestic asset price boom would have made monetary restraint the desirable policy option.

[13]Capital mobility, interdependence, and the globalization of the world's financial markets are increasingly making the notion of a truly "independent" monetary policy more a theoretical proposition than a policy option. On this point Schwartz (1993, p. 172) notes: "Central banks of the industrialized countries themselves no longer believe that they know how to produce monetary surprises that are stabilizing and that they are masters of discretion." Nevertheless, it is legitimate to speak of a relatively less constrained monetary policy as might happen outside the context of a CBA (e.g., Latvia).

[14]The average ratio of broad money to GDP in the Baltic countries in 1996 was 20 percent, ranging from 13 percent in Lithuania to 27 percent in Estonia. The same unweighted ratio for a sample of seven small open European countries (Austria, Belgium, Denmark, Finland, Norway, Sweden, and Switzerland) in 1995 was 69 percent.

currency means that the central bank cannot be the lender of last resort for the banking system. Indeed, a view has been put forward that there is an implicit trade off between the lower convertibility risk under a CBA and the possibly higher risk of a domestic financial crisis since an increase in the demand for cash will lead to a contraction of the banking system. (Indeed, in Lithuania, during the first three months of the banking crisis—that is, the first quarter of 1996—the CBA converted sufficient currency into foreign exchange to lead to a contraction in reserve money and broad money, the latter on the order of 13 percent). CBAs have dealt with these risks partly by creating a separate bailout facility that is allowed to provide limited assistance, within the constraints imposed by the excess over the minimum amount required for backing. Unless the cushion of such "excess" foreign reserves is substantial, the CBA's ability to respond to a major financial crisis will be sharply circumscribed. Indeed, an argument often put forward in favor of a conventional peg (as opposed to a CBA) stems from the potential fragility of the domestic banking system in the absence of a lender of last resort and the possibility that a liquidity crisis could turn into a systemic crisis affecting the banking system.[15]

The CBAs in Estonia and Lithuania have withstood reasonably well these countries' respective banking crises, both of which originated in the context of ineffective supervision and poor banking practices (weak lending skills, insider abuse, overextension of the banks' branch network, violations of regulatory provisions, undercapitalization, among others) and both of which eventually resulted in the closing or restructuring of a number of problem banks. Some central bank lending took place in the context of operations to relieve liquidity problems, but this was limited and the costs of bank restructuring were rapidly transferred (or are in the process of being transferred) to the budget.[16]

A case can be made that the presence of the CBAs during the banking crises (or the authorities' firm commitment to the peg in Latvia), rather than acting as a serious constraint, may have played the role of a hard budget constraint, sharply limiting the room for maneuver of the government at a time when the

temptation to relax policies in the face of strong political pressures was great. By forcing the closure or restructuring of the banking system's worst offenders and focusing the authorities' attention on some of the underlying weaknesses and the need for reforms, the CBAs may have actually contributed to improving the medium-term viability of the banking system. The CBAs in the Baltic countries have also lessened the extent of the moral hazard problem implicit in a system with a central bank legally able—and perhaps quite willing—to act as a lender of last resort. On the other hand, the outcome of these particular episodes does not prove the more general case that the absence of the lender-of-last-resort function would also be beneficial in future episodes of banking difficulties.

The banking crises have prompted the introduction of medium-term strategies for restructuring the banking sectors, involving, inter alia, tighter prudential rules and international accounting standards, improved monitoring of banks, recapitalization or privatization of former state-owned problem banks, and the introduction of private deposit insurance schemes. Nevertheless, the possibility of future crises cannot be ruled out. Short of an active use of excess holdings of foreign exchange for lender-of-last-resort or monetary operations (which would run counter to the basic premise of a CBA of limited discretion), a case can be made that "some flexibility can add to the sustainability of a currency board and thus enhance its credibility." Indeed, "institutional arrangements, operational procedures and monetary and prudential instruments can be designed to reduce risks of a systemic liquidity crisis while limiting discretionary interference from the monetary authorities. In addition, public debt policies can be reformed to limit the risk of a debt crisis. Nevertheless, some lender-of-last-resort support is needed—preferably under central bank control—to contain financial sector problems at an early stage and avert contagion risks. This should be done in a manner that addresses systemic problems in the banking system while seeking to avoid bailouts of insolvent banks. Indeed, the existence of such support facilities can enhance confidence in the domestic financial system, and hence lower intermediation spreads."[17]

Fiscal Discipline

The limited scope (de facto or de jure) for monetary and exchange rate policies in the Baltics puts a considerably greater burden on fiscal policy in support of the authorities' macroeconomic and stabilization objectives. It also raises the issue of the extent

---

[15]Actually, two additional features that can help alleviate such pressures would be the presence of a well-developed interbank money market and the presence of foreign banks in the domestic market that could draw upon resources of their parent banks. Neither of these options is yet readily available in the Baltic countries, at least not in a way that might make a tangible difference.

[16]In Lithuania, for instance, loans granted by the Bank of Lithuania to the State Commercial Bank in July–August 1996 were repaid in September 1996, thereby fully restoring the lender of last resort margin under the program's net international reserves target.

---

[17]See Baliño (1997).

to which the CBAs have contributed in a tangible way to greater fiscal discipline and whether, in the absence of a commitment to sound fiscal policies, a CBA or fixed rate regime could actually generate it. With few exceptions (Latvia in 1995, Lithuania in 1994, and Estonia in 1996), the Baltics have built a favorable track record of fiscal discipline, and the commitment to a fixed exchange rate has contributed to reinforce that record. By constraining the financing options available to the government, the CBAs have imposed a harder budget constraint than would otherwise have been the case (e.g., by allowing the closure of problem banks, budget support for bank restructuring may turn out to be less costly than would have been the case had the government been able to monetize a large budget deficit) and thus buttressed the authorities' anti-inflation policies.

Portfolio Constraints

In reviewing the role of currency boards, Schwartz (1993) notes the criticisms made early on in the debate of their relative costs and merits on account of the need to fully back the monetary base by foreign currency. It was argued that since it was highly unlikely that the entire currency issue would have to be redeemed at one time, maintaining the equivalent of a 100+ percent reserve requirement was unduly limiting, possibly denying the monetary authorities (and ultimately the government) more profitable investment opportunities.[18] A measure of the seigniorage lost via a currency board would have to take due account of the risk-adjusted yield on domestic assets when compared with the yield on the foreign assets that they would be replacing, as well as other, possibly distortionary, effects associated with, for instance, monetization of government deficits.[19] In practice, a case can be made that the seigniorage "losses" in the Baltic CBAs are minimal (if not zero), since, in any event, the reserves held as coverage for the currency issue are at about the levels that they should be (about three months' worth of imports) for small, relatively open economies, even if the country in question did not have a currency board. Moreover, from market participants' point of view, it is likely that a high coverage ratio (even in excess of the amount of central bank domestic liabilities) would be perceived as enhancing credibility of the underlying arrangement, since it would leave the central bank room to deal with a banking crisis. It

also needs to be noted that the sole reliance on balance of payments flows to supply the monetary base may make adjustment to changes in money demand more severe than necessary.

Solvency Risks

Regardless of the particular exchange rate regime, in a typical banking system balance sheet, assets and liabilities denominated in both the local and the reserve currency coexist. The full convertibility of the domestic currency under a CBA implies that the banking system must be able to convert, on demand, its liabilities in domestic currency into the reserve currency. If the exchange rate peg is perfectly credible, the coexistence of liabilities denominated in two different currencies does not introduce any additional solvency risk. If, however, there is a sudden change in sentiment concerning the government's commitment to the fixed rate (or the underlying institutional arrangements), the resulting rise in the interest rate paid on domestic currency denominated assets will depress the market value of the banks' long-term domestic currency assets. Given the fixed exchange rate, the reduction in the market value of banks' assets will not be matched by a reduction in the value of their short-run domestic currency liabilities. This implies that a CBA with such a mixed banking system balance sheet could be subject to changes in asset valuation driven by changes in exchange rate expectations. While this may not be a serious problem in practice (since CBAs reinforce credibility in the parity) it can be an occasional source of potential instability (e.g., the arrival of a new government that the market perceives as being less committed to maintaining the CBA) and can be eliminated only by denominating the entire balance sheet of the banking system in the reserve currency; that is, complete "dollarization," or by maintaining complete credibility at all times.[20]

Policy Options Over the Medium Term

This section analyzes some of the limitations (potential or otherwise) associated with the Baltic countries' approach to exchange rate management and briefly discusses the sustainability of the underlying arrangements.

---

[18]Considerations of this type may be behind calls, voiced occasionally, for more active use of foreign reserves in support of domestic economic activity.

[19]Osband and Villanueva (1993) note that revenue from seigniorage stems from the interest earned on investing the foreign reserves *minus* the "costs of printing bank notes and minting coins."

---

[20]The issue is more complicated, since while the banks can protect themselves against the exchange rate risk by reducing their open position, they cannot protect themselves against the risk that their loans will go bad if their customers are adversely affected by an exchange rate change.

Choice of Exchange Rate Regime

Any assessment of options for monetary and exchange rate policies over the medium term should take into account the Baltic countries' stated intentions to join the EU, a goal for which there appears to be a broad-based domestic consensus. Integration with the EU and the process leading to eventual accession will provide a clearly defined framework over the medium term for the conduct of economic policies, as evidenced, for instance, by ongoing broad-based efforts in a large number of areas to adapt institutions and legislation to the standards prevailing in the EU. In this respect, clear evidence of sustained commitment to a stable exchange rate and the policies that support it, as demonstrated, for instance, by the institutional ability to stick to a simple monetary rule (or one involving, as in Latvia, limited effective discretion) and the willingness and readiness to cede some sovereignty in specified areas are conditions that could facilitate the process of integration with the EU.

It was noted recently that "the choice of exchange rate regime is one of the longest-running debates in economics," and "the fact that it is not resolved must mean that there is no exchange rate system that is superior in all circumstances."[21] Early discussion in the literature argued that pegging would be beneficial if the degree of factor mobility (regional and interindustry) was appropriately high, the size of the economy relatively small, and the degree of openness sufficiently high.[22] With the possible exception of relative factor mobility (on which the empirical evidence is lacking), the Baltic countries are certainly small and relatively open, suggesting the desirability of a fixed rate regime. As noted earlier, credibly pegging to a stable currency or basket of currencies of low-inflation countries does ensure a transition to lower inflation. In particular, as pointed out by Fischer: "it helps focus the mind of the government on a very clear constraint on policy" (p. 36).

Beyond issues of the structure of the economy (e.g., relative size, degree of openness) and credibility, a key consideration that argues in favor of a fixed exchange rate in the Baltic countries stems from their governments' determination to seek membership in the EU and, eventually, its monetary arrangements. Since EMU entry criteria are likely to require a prolonged period of exchange rate stability vis-à-

vis the euro, a temporary switch to more flexible arrangements to be followed by a return to a fixed regime might seem unnecessary. With these and other considerations in mind, the Bank of Lithuania, for instance, has recently begun to implement a medium-term strategy for the gradual evolution of the CBA into a traditional peg, such as presently exists in Latvia and that, in its final stage, envisages a permanent fixing of the rate vis-à-vis the euro (see Appendix I for details). This approach raises a number of interesting policy issues; some are identified and discussed below.

Because of the tougher institutional arrangements associated with a CBA, market participants typically perceive that the probability of a change in the exchange rate under a conventional peg is higher. Other things being equal, this lower credibility would normally be associated with a higher level of interest rates under a peg. Furthermore, maintaining a fixed rate in the context of financial liberalization can raise some difficulties. Pursuit of a tight money policy to reduce inflation may push domestic interest rates above foreign rates and lead to capital inflows, which may offset the effects of the tight monetary policy. Unless the source of the inflow is an increase in the domestic demand for money (in which case the appropriate response is to allow the money supply to rise), such capital inflows can exert pressures on the exchange rate.

A key difference between a CBA and a fixed exchange rate regime pertains to the possibility of sterilized intervention. Under a conventional peg the central bank may allow an increase in foreign reserves while maintaining the money supply constant. Under a CBA, the monetary authorities cannot, through purchases of domestic currency bonds, sterilize the potentially contractionary effect on the domestic money base associated with sales of foreign exchange.[23] Sterilized intervention can thus, in principle, smooth out such temporary shocks and may allow the monetary authorities to partly neutralize the effects of capital inflows.[24]

An argument sometimes made against fixing the exchange rate is that it can reduce the authorities' room for maneuver during macroeconomic shocks. A real shock (e.g., a sharp increase in the price of imported oil, as occurred in the Baltic countries in 1991/92) will require adjustments in relative prices—like the real exchange rate—and the absence

---

[21]Fischer (1996), p. 36.

[22]For an introductory survey see Isard (1995). A discussion of the relationship between relative size and openness and the effectiveness of a given devaluation of the exchange rate is presented in Tower and Willett (1976). A number of arguments are put forward there as to why exchange rate adjustment is relatively less effective in small, open, undiversified economies, than in large, closed ones.

[23]For instance, reserve money fell by 20 percent in Lithuania between December 1995 and March 1996, in the aftermath of the banking crisis.

[24]In this regard, Fischer (1996) also notes the virtues of fiscal discipline and the fact that some countries have sometimes successfully implemented "market-based policies to reduce the returns to foreign investors" (e.g., via increases in reserve requirements on nonresident deposits or other temporary measures).

of sufficient flexibility in the domestic price level in the short run will mean that flexibility in the nominal exchange rate will make it easier to achieve the desired level in the real rate. The literature on optimal currency areas suggests that the choice of the exchange regime should recognize the existence of unpredictable and persistent shocks, and that the decision to join a currency area should entail careful analysis of the nature of the underlying shocks and of their degree of symmetry. Other things being equal, the more asymmetric the distribution of real shocks across countries, the greater the country's cost of forgoing the option of exchange rate adjustment. Since the process of convergence between the Baltics and their trade partners (particularly in the EU) is far from complete, the possibility cannot be excluded that some real shocks might arise requiring a terms of trade adjustment and an exchange rate realignment. Should the Baltic countries succeed in keeping their labor markets flexible, even after EU accession, then the costs of these future shocks would not be magnified by the presence of a fixed exchange rate.

Whether the monetary authorities operate under a CBA or a traditional peg has important implications for the role that they may play in accelerating the deepening of financial markets and, more generally, encouraging institutional development. As will be argued below, the Baltic countries need to make further progress in this area, particularly in the banking sector and in enhancing the sophistication and flexibility of financial markets. Under a narrow and strict definition of a CBA, the monetary authorities can play only a limited role in these institutional processes. Partly to address some of these limitations and as a first step in a process aimed at broadening the development of other monetary instruments over the medium term, the Bank of Lithuania started limited repurchase operations on treasury bills as a way of facilitating the development of the secondary market, which has remained thin, illiquid, and noncompetitive (see Appendix I).

Preconditions for a Switch

If a country decides to make the switch from a CBA to a conventional peg, a key issue concerns the conditions that need to be in place to ensure a successful transition. This section identifies and examines the relevance of a number of such factors for the Baltic countries. In particular, the focus is on the role and underlying strength of the banking system, the development of the domestic financial markets, and the adequacy of the level of foreign exchange reserves. Central bank independence and the existence of a clear mandate to enforce price stability as well as the need to develop a sufficient degree of institu-

tional capacity for the exercise of the necessary functions are also discussed. While the factors identified here are all desirable policy objectives and, to a greater or lesser degree, should be pursued independently of the exchange rate regime, they acquire particular relevance (as will be noted below) in the context of transition economies characterized by structural rigidities and inefficiencies, particularly in the financial sector.

Strength of the Banking System

In the Baltics, as in other countries, the implementation of monetary policy requires the existence of relatively stable relationships between instruments and policy objectives. Disruptions to the financial system adversely affect these relationships and the links between policy instruments (e.g., interest rates, money, and credit aggregates) and policy objectives, such as price stability. Regardless of whether monetary policy is transmitted through direct or indirect instruments, the transmission mechanism is closely linked to and ultimately depends upon the soundness of the banking system. Indirect instruments of monetary policy will be affected adversely by illiquid or insolvent banks, because of their inability to adjust reserves or lending in response to monetary policy signals. Banks with limited balance sheet flexibility may not be able to respond appropriately to policy changes; for example, reserve requirements will not be effective if illiquid banks are not able to meet them. A credit auction or similar market-based liquidity facility may be distorted by adverse selection and moral hazard, since unsound institutions may be willing to borrow at any price to avoid illiquidity. If high-risk borrowers represent a substantial share of total commercial bank credit, the effectiveness of liquidity management through open market operations will be reduced by the low interest-rate elasticity of banks' credit demand. Similarly, when the authorities employ direct policy instruments, such as credit ceilings, their effectiveness will be reduced if weak banks simply rollover their portfolio of bad loans or if the liquidity provided by new deposits goes to finance banks' losses on nonperforming loans. In such cases, credit ceilings will not be especially effective in constraining the growth of net domestic assets (NDA) of the banking system.

The strengthening of confidence in the banking sector in turn is essential to the widening and deepening of financial markets. As a result of the banking crises in Latvia and Lithuania, nominal interest rates rose sharply and did not begin to fall appreciably until the strengthened enforcement of prudential banking regulations and the beginning of the implementation of bank restructuring programs. Similarly, the laying out of solid foundations for the development of the capital markets depends on an appropriate, consistent legal framework that clearly lays out the "rules of the game" in the financial sector and in the interactions of the financial sector with the rest of the economy (e.g., collateral). Without a consistent and transparent set of laws, the risk premium will be high and investors will not invest domestically. These structures have only been recently put in place in all three Baltic countries and, as a result, nominal interest rates have come down. It remains to be seen whether the bank restructuring strategies will ultimately be successful (particularly in Latvia and Lithuania) and at what (fiscal) cost. Further strengthening of the banking system and the underlying regulatory climate would be a desirable policy objective in terms of the institutional developments that must take place ahead of EU accession.

Central Bank Independence

In Lithuania (as in Estonia and Latvia), the Law on the Bank of Lithuania recognizes the central bank as an institution "independent from the Government of the Republic of Lithuania and other institutions of executive authority" and it explicitly states that its "principal objective is to achieve stability of the currency." The bank is called upon to support the government's overall economic policy, "provided said policy is in compliance with the principal objective of the Bank." The governor is appointed by parliament (for a period of five years in Lithuania[25]) and cannot be dismissed prior to the expiration of his or her term, unless he or she is convicted of some crime or is not able to perform his or her duties properly due to health problems. From a legal point of view, the basis for an independent monetary policy appears to be well established in the Baltic countries.

Nevertheless, the sequence of events that led to the resignation of the governor of the Bank of Lithuania at the peak of the banking crisis in the spring of 1996 raises questions about a possible gap between the de jure independence of the central bank and the effective interpretation and implementation of that law in practice.[26] In general, the literature on central bank independence notes that an otherwise legally independent central bank will maintain its

credibility only as long as it operates in a political environment where support for the idea of using monetary policy for the medium-term control of inflation is broad-based, where the track record of adherence to the rule of law is reasonably long and where, more generally, the legal climate is characterized by stability and predictability. Given the early stages of the transition in the Baltic countries, the ample scope for further progress in a number of areas, particularly on the structural front, as well as the need to continue to build up public support for macroeconomic stability and a free market, including the need to generate a broader consensus on the role of medium-term targets for monetary policy, an appropriate legal, institutional, and public opinion context for the exercise of an adequately independent monetary policy may not yet exist in Lithuania. However, there is consensus that the Latvian and Estonian central banks, while operating in a broadly similar formal legal climate as in Lithuania, enjoy a higher degree of effective independence.[27]

Gross Reserves and Central Bank Liabilities

In assessing the adequacy of foreign reserves in a transition economy, it is desirable to consider the underlying policy environment, as well as the level and structure of liabilities of the central bank. The experience of several countries in recent years suggests that foreign exchange flows can exhibit significant volatility in the presence of uncertainties associated with, for instance, perceptions about the policies of a newly elected government or other, more systemic, factors. At the peak of the banking crisis in Lithuania, for instance, foreign exchange outflows through the CBA during a two-month period reached nearly $150 million (equivalent to some 17 percent of gross reserves prior to the crisis).

The gross reserve positions of the three Baltic countries are shown in Table 3.1. These are in the neighborhood of 2½–3½ months of imports. Because the monetary authorities have significant foreign liabilities (e.g., $350 million in Lithuania, of which 90 percent are to the IMF), the *net* foreign asset positions are lower and range over 1½–2½ months of imports. For a small, relatively open, market economy, gross reserves equivalent to some three months of imports have typically been considered adequate. The need to further strengthen the domestic financial systems in all three countries and the underlying uncertainties associated with the early

---

[25]Article 10 of the Law states that "The chairperson . . . shall be appointed for a term of five years and his or her salary shall be fixed by the Seimas of the Republic of Lithuania upon the recommendation of the President of the Republic." The law does not spell out in detail the procedures for appointing the chairperson, however.

[26]In early 1996, following the imposition of moratoriums on several large insolvent banks, the Board and the top management of the bank were forced to resign. The present incumbent is the fifth governor the bank has had during the six-year period through 1997.

[27]It may be recalled that in Latvia in 1995, following the closure of Bank Baltija, a motion of no confidence in the governor and deputy governor of the central bank was introduced in parliament; in the event, the motion failed. It is not clear what would have been its legal status, had it succeeded.

stages of the transition (in particular, the need to continue to support the convergence of inflation with respect to regional partners in the EU and to accelerate the process of structural reforms), suggest that a more cautious approach is desirable, calling for a wider margin of safety, that is, a relatively high reserve coverage ratio.

Secondary Market for Treasury Bills and Interbank Lending

An important condition for the adoption of indirect policy instruments is a well-functioning money market that continuously transmits to the authorities up-to-date information on liquidity conditions and interest rate developments. In Latvia and Lithuania, while the primary market for treasury bills has developed rapidly, secondary trading of treasury securities has remained quite limited, with estimated annual turnover on the order of 10–15 percent of the stock of the securities issued. There are several reasons for the thin secondary trading. First, financial institutions are not capable of operating as market makers, either because they have insufficient capital (in the case of brokerage companies) or because they lack the experience and the relevant skills. Second, the actual number of participants is usually very small. Last, in Lithuania, taxation is a limiting factor as capital gains taxes are paid only on securities that are sold before maturity.

Except for Estonia, the interbank market is similarly underdeveloped. In Lithuania, the market collapsed in late 1995 and has not recovered despite government guarantees, registering only a few transactions a week. It is unlikely that before bank restructuring actually takes place and the public regains full confidence in the system, a secondary market for bank reserves that is liquid, deep, and capable of signaling to the authorities interest rate developments will come into existence.

Institutional Development

Institutional capacity for the conduct of monetary policy is difficult to measure. In Estonia and Lithuania, the problem is further complicated since there is no way of using past policy performance as an indicator of institutional strength even though the two central banks have had available to them limited lender-of-last-resort functions, mainly intended to preserve the viability of the banking system. The amounts of financial resources that are, in principle, available to the central banks of Estonia and Lithuania to fulfill lender-of-last-resort functions are not insignificant. One can think of two types of margins for the available resources: those established with respect to the program limits (i.e., floors on net inter-

national reserves), which are relatively narrow (1.6 percent and 10 percent of reserve money, respectively). The more fundamental limits are implicit in the requirement of 100 percent cover for reserve money; since actual cover is greater than 100 percent, excess resources that could be used for lender-of-last-resort operations without violating the cover requirement amount to 37 percent and 30 percent of reserve money, respectively.

Under the simple monetary rules of CBAs, the day-to-day conduct of monetary policy does not hinge to any crucial degree on the availability of up-to-date information on total liquidity, nor does it require, as a matter of high priority, the development of a sophisticated forecast capacity and other analytical skills within the central banks. If alternative exchange rate arrangements are to be pursued at some point in the future, the development of the relevant research and analytical functions of the central bank would become an indispensable institutional requirement. Both central banks have made some limited headway in this area; in Lithuania a research division was recently created to prepare short-term forecasts for reserve money, while at the Bank of Estonia the research department produces macroeconomic forecasts for real variables and analyzes monetary developments but is not involved in the preparation of periodic monetary and interest rate projections.

There is obviously scope for the development of additional institutional capacities in the area of monetary instruments, such as open market operations, rediscount facilities, credit auctions, and so on, as in Latvia. The problem is that conventional open market and credit operations go against the spirit of a currency board and are essentially ruled out in the context of the present policy framework. In this regard, the development of these capacities would appear to require the introduction of a transition period during which some measure of flexibility is introduced in the arrangements.[28]

Conclusions

This section has reviewed the recent experience of the Baltic countries with fixed exchange rate regimes, currency boards in Estonia and Lithuania, and a peg to the SDR in Latvia that has involved little de facto use of monetary policy instruments. Against a background of declining inflation and falling interest rates, along with a recovery of output and a strengthened balance of payments position in all three countries, the section has argued that the ex-

---

[28]Some elaboration on the kinds of operations that could be developed as a country shifts to a policy involving somewhat greater discretion than under a CBA is presented in Appendix II.

isting arrangements have served the authorities' stabilization policies well, having backed the credibility of stabilization through an institutional anchoring of financial restraint.

The potential disadvantages sometimes associated with fixed exchange rate regimes (and in particular with CBAs), such as the risks of overvaluation, vulnerability to shocks, and the absence of a lender of last resort, do not appear, on balance, to have constrained the implementation of credible macroeconomic policies in the Baltic countries and may, in some circumstances, have actually reinforced the authorities' determination to pursue tight policies in the face of strong political pressures to do otherwise. On the basis of the evidence, no compelling case can be made that it is necessary at the present time to change in a fundamental way the approach to exchange rate management in the Baltic countries. In addition, the Baltic countries' stated intention to integrate their economies with the EU, and the policy requirements that this process is likely to entail, would argue in favor of a commitment to a stable exchange rate and the policies that support it.

The relative success to date of the fundamental policy framework in place for the Baltic states should not preclude the consideration of alternative arrangements. Alternative policy scenarios, involving greater flexibility in the conduct of monetary policy, should be developed and kept under review especially given the changing global environment.

Appendix I. The CBA and an Exit Strategy

In January 1997, the Bank of Lithuania completed a medium-term policy paper that lays out a strategy for the gradual evolution of the currency board arrangement into a traditional currency peg. The basic objective underlying the strategy is the strengthening of political and economic links with the EU, including eventual membership and participation in its monetary institutions. The strategy distinguishes clearly the institutional arrangements underlying the CBA and, in particular, the automatic creation of a monetary base associated with foreign exchange inflows, and the choice of a fixed exchange rate regime per se. The program envisages three stages:

(1) The first stage began in 1997. The Bank of Lithuania would keep the CBA in place but gradually introduce new monetary policy instruments, within the room permitted under the ceilings of the program under the Extended Financing Facility. The instruments introduced were repurchase operations in treasury bills and a short-term Lombard credit fa-

cility, collateralized by treasury bills. The bank committed itself to limiting the amount of repurchase operations held in its balance sheet to LTL 60 million and to clear the balance of such operations periodically. The provisions were designed to ensure that an adequate margin would be maintained for the lender-of-last-resort function. The Lombard facility would be a standard credit window for commercial banks and, in contrast with the existing liquidity loans, would have the advantage of being collateralized with short-term assets rather than being guaranteed by the government.

(2) During the second stage, which, originally, was to start in early 1998, the government would introduce amendments to the Litas Stability Law, allowing a broadening of the definition of the assets that could be used to back reserve money. While this would alter the essential character of the CBA, under which central bank liabilities may be backed only by foreign exchange reserves, the authorities would like to retain the Litas Stability Law itself, since its various features contribute to confidence (e.g., article 4 of the law, which ensures full convertibility of the domestic currency). With a view to further buttressing confidence in the currency, the existing parity with the dollar would be maintained and the foreign exchange position of the Bank of Lithuania would be strengthened. It would be ready to conduct sterilized interventions, as needed.

(3) In the third and final stage, to be introduced not earlier than 1999, the litas exchange rate would be pegged to a basket made up of the U.S. dollar and the euro, should the latter be in existence, or some other basket of EU currencies. Necessary conditions for entering the final stage of the program would be a monthly rate of inflation below 0.8 percent for a period of six consecutive months and substantial growth in banking sector deposits. This stage would precede the permanent fixing of the rate vis-à-vis the euro.

Appendix II. Monetary Policy Instruments During Transition

The transition from a CBA to a conventional peg—if this were the path chosen—would be accompanied by a shift in the underlying institutional arrangements and a gradual introduction of the monetary instruments currently unavailable to the central banks in Estonia and Lithuania.[29] This appendix dis-

---

[29]The Estonian authorities have publicly stated that they do not envisage any change to the currency board and the present peg, except with the advent of the European Monetary Union when the kroon's link to the deutsche mark will be replaced by a link to the euro according to the conversion rate at which the value of the deutsche mark will be fixed to the euro.

cusses possibilities in this area, some of which could start without any changes to underlying legislation.

First, the central bank could engage in activities aimed at stimulating the development of the weak interbank markets. With particular reference to Lithuania, the central bank could encourage commercial banks to shift, on an overnight basis, excess reserves across accounts, thus helping improve daily management of reserves. By operating as an overnight broker, the bank would not create additional liquidity and would not be involved in any risk of default or exchange risk. The Bank of Estonia also holds excess reserves but, given the substantial development of the interbank market there, the need for a central bank brokerage role is certainly less urgent.

Second, the central banks could marginally expand available discretionary net domestic asset margins, thus creating the opportunity for a broadening of the central bank's institutional experience, under an otherwise controlled environment. The discretionary margin, currently viewed as a margin of last resort, would be available for open market and credit operations.[30] An obvious instrument available to the authorities under this option would be repurchase operations in some liquid short-term asset, such as treasury bills in Lithuania and central bank certificates of deposit in Estonia. Another instrument that could be developed would be a credit auction facility, similar to the one that existed, for example, in Lithuania before the introduction of the CBA.[31] Credit auctions can be a way of pricing central bank credit at this stage in the development of the money market and the absence of a reliable interbank reference rate. Credit auctions would need to be collateralized; in Lithuania, with the ample availability of treasury bills, a natural collateral is already available. In the medium term, central banks could gradually introduce a standard credit facility, against the collateral of eligible bills. The development of a well-developed interbank market would provide a natural reference interest rate and would make it possible to introduce directly a standard discount window.

A third way to introduce further flexibility in the CBA would be to allow a small portion of the foreign reserve backing for the monetary base to be made up of government bonds denominated in convertible currency, as in Argentina. This alternative would create additional opportunities for conducting open market operations that could be used to smooth out intramonthly fluctuations in the demand for cash.[32]

The combination of the above options involving degrees of flexibility appropriately tailored to each country's particular institutional circumstances and preferences would make it possible over time to gradually replace the conventional CBA by a traditional peg. To reduce the possibility of a heightening of tensions in the financial markets the process of changing the legislative framework would need to be managed carefully.

References

Baliño, Tomás, Charles Enoch, and others, 1997, *Currency Board Arrangements—Issues and Experiences,* IMF Occasional Paper No. 151 (Washington: International Monetary Fund).

Bennett, Adam G., 1994, "Currency Boards: Issues and Experiences," IMF Paper on Policy Analysis and Assessment 94/18 (Washington: International Monetary Fund).

Berengaut, Julian, and others, 1996, *Republic of Lithuania—Recent Economic Developments,* IMF Staff Country Report No. 96/72 (Washington: International Monetary Fund).

Camard, Wayne, 1996, "Discretion with Rules? Lessons from the Currency Board Arrangement in Lithuania," IMF Paper on Policy Analysis and Assessment 96/1 (Washington: International Monetary Fund).

Citrin, D.A., and A.K. Lahiri, 1995, *Policy Experiences and Issues in the Baltics, Russia, and Other Countries of the Former Soviet Union,* IMF Occasional Paper No. 133 (Washington: International Monetary Fund).

Caprio, G., M. Dooley, D. Leipziger, and C. Walsh, 1996, "The Lender of Last Resort Function Under a Currency Board," Policy Research Working Paper No. 1648 (Washington: World Bank).

Engel, Charles, and John H. Rogers, 1996, "How Wide Is the Border?" *American Economic Review,* Vol. 86, (December), pp. 1112–25.

Fischer, Stanley, 1996, "Maintaining Price Stability," *Finance & Development,* Vol. 33 (December 1996), pp. 34–37.

Halpern, L., and C. Wyplosz, 1996, "Equilibrium Exchange Rates in Transition Economies," IMF Working Paper 96/125 (Washington: International Monetary Fund).

Isard, Peter, 1995, *Exchange Rate Economics* (Cambridge: Cambridge University Press).

Lorie, Henri, and others, 1996, *Republic of Estonia—Selected Issues and Statistical Appendix,* IMF Staff Country Report No. 96/96 (Washington: International Monetary Fund).

---

[30]To protect the lender-of-last-resort function, at least partial clearance of the facilities might be required on a periodic basis.

[31]The authorities would need to carefully explain to economic agents that these credit auctions are conducted with "surplus" resources and, as such, would not compromise the CBA.

---

[32]The Litas Stability Law, for instance, includes in the definition of foreign exchange reserves "bonds, and other debt securities payable in convertible currency, which are held by the Bank of Lithuania." This would not appear to preclude the introduction of such domestic bonds denominated in a convertible currency.

Osband, K., and D. Villanueva, 1993, "Independent Currency Authorities: An Analytic Primer," *Staff Papers,* International Monetary Fund, Vol. 40 (March), pp. 202–16.

Parsley, David C., and Shang-Jin Wei, 1996, "Convergence to the Law of One Price Without Trade Barriers or Currency Fluctuations," *Quarterly Journal of Economics* (November), pp. 1211–36.

Richards, A., and G. Tersman, 1995, "Growth, Nontradables, and Price Convergence in the Baltics," IMF Working Paper 95/45 (Washington: International Monetary Fund).

Rogoff, Kenneth, 1996, "The Purchasing Power Parity Puzzle," *Journal of Economic Literature,* Vol. 34 (June), pp. 647–68.

Schwartz, Anna, 1993, "Currency Boards: Their Past, Present, and Possible Future Role," *Carnegie-Rochester Conference Series on Public Policy,* Vol. 39, pp. 147–87.

Tower, E., and T.D. Willett, 1976, "The Theory of Optimum Currency Areas and Exchange Rate Flexibility," *Special Papers in International Economics* (Princeton University: International Finance Section).

Saavalainen, Tapio O., 1995, "Stabilization in the Baltic Countries: Early Experience," *Road Maps of the Transition,* IMF Occasional Paper No. 127 (Washington: International Monetary Fund).

van der Mensbrugghe, Emmanuel, and others, 1996, *Republic of Latvia—Recent Economic Developments,* IMF Staff Country Report No. 96/143 (Washington: International Monetary Fund).

Williamson, John, 1995, *What Role for Currency Boards?* (Washington: Institute for International Economics, September).

IV Fiscal Issues

Dennis Jones and Françoise Le Gall

The fiscal issues that are of particular interest to transition economies broadly center on the role that government should play in the transition from a planned to a market economy. A key question in this regard is, "Where do the Baltic countries appear to be heading?" Resolute rejection of Soviet practices and a commitment to join the European Union imply that the Baltics are moving toward western European models of economic and financial development and that they will tend to develop institutional arrangements and policies similar to those among their Scandinavian and continental European neighbors. This may especially be true in fiscal management, given the Baltic countries' wish to comply fully with the Maastricht guidelines and, more generally, their desire to adapt their policies and institutions to the requirements of EU membership. Notwithstanding the progress that they have made in carrying out market-oriented reforms, they are not as far along the road as the more successful early transition economies (e.g., the Czech Republic, Poland, and Hungary).[1] Their underlying institutional base is still much weaker than in the EU and considerable change is required to meet its standards.

Fiscal policy has already taken center stage in the Baltics' economic policies, largely because these countries have adopted fixed exchange rate regimes that give limited scope to active use of monetary instruments. In common with other transition economies, the Baltics initially faced the dual task of keeping their fiscal deficits compatible with macroeconomic stabilization objectives and of creating room for private initiative by reducing state involvement in the economy (reducing the size of government, raising revenue in a less distortionary manner, and improving the expenditure mix). The authorities have shown a strong commitment to fiscal discipline and, following the early transition period, achieved broad macroeconomic stabilization.

While the economies have undergone rapid and creditable transformation, the scope of the required fiscal reforms means that relative progress in this area has been somewhat slower. In keeping with most transition economies, the Baltics were quick to change major taxes, for example, abandoning turnover taxes and residual enterprise profit transfers in favor of western-style value-added taxes, personal income taxes, and parametric profit taxes. These changes, in conjunction with a strong starting position on the fiscal accounts, helped the Baltics avoid the sharp revenue decline that was evident in most republics of the Commonwealth of Independent States (CIS). Among expenditure reforms, price subsidies were either quickly removed or substantially reduced. However, there are a number of important expenditure reforms that are necessary but politically and administratively complex to implement.

Fiscal reforms in the Baltics would yield two principal benefits. First, they would facilitate economic stabilization, and thus help improve prospects for long-term economic growth, particularly in fostering an economic environment conducive to private saving and investment.[2] Growth is likely to be enhanced by well-planned public spending aimed at building market-based institutions, strengthening government administration, improving physical infrastructure, and setting up a viable social safety net (Fischer, Sahay, and Végh). Second, over the medium term, they could contribute to the development of sustainable fiscal policies.

Fiscal reform will involve both policies and institutions. The main focus of reform needs to be on strengthening the budget processes; maintaining the current high degree of revenue mobilization; and re-examining expenditure priorities. On the latter, there is a pressing need to reassess social safety net provisions, notably pensions as these are already exerting heavy pressure on public finances.[3]

The remainder of this section will look briefly at progress to date in each of these three areas and outline the main challenges facing the Baltic countries.

---

[1]See IMF (1996b), and Fischer, Sahay, and Végh (1998).

[2]See IMF (1996b).

[3]This focus is not meant to ignore the fact that there are other important issues to consider regarding expenditure management, such as the need to rationalize education and health expenditure, and to adequately protect capital expenditure.

Budget Processes

Substantial reform of public sector financial management in the Baltics is an important part of their transition to market economies. Expenditure management reforms would help move policies away from ad hoc expenditure cuts and improve the allocation of public resources, in particular toward projects and activities that continue the process of economic restructuring and promote economic growth. These reforms will involve both budget preparation and execution.

The literature on budget processes notes that (hierarchical and) transparent procedures are associated with greater fiscal discipline, especially when more power is concentrated with the treasury than with spending ministries, and the role of parliament is limited to amending the budget proposed by the government.[4]

Overview of Budget Procedures

The constitutions and budget laws set the legal framework for budget formulation in each of the Baltic states. These pieces of legislation define the institutional coverage of the national and local budgets, and the main legislative procedures for their approval. The procedures and timetables for budget approval seem to be clear in all three countries. Each has provisions for the draft national budget to be submitted for approval some three months before the start of the new fiscal year. Supplementary provisions cover the eventuality that a new budget may not be approved on time and call for monthly expenditure to continue at the rate of one-twelfth of the allocation of the last approved budget. Since the introduction of new budget laws at the start of the transition, there have been no major changes in any of the countries in the structure and form of budget procedures.

Each country has a different view of what constitutes the official national budget.[5] In Estonia, parliament approves the "state" budget, which covers central government, and the Social Insurance and Medical Insurance Funds. The state budget must be balanced, with revenue matching expenditure as defined in the budget laws (these classify a drawdown of bank deposits as revenue). In Latvia, parliament approves a budget for the central government and national extrabudgetary funds. The budget may have a deficit to be covered by various forms of domestic and foreign financing. In Lithuania, the "state" budget approved by parliament covers only central government operations, and the budget may include a deficit and associated domestic and foreign financing.

In each of the Baltics, the role of parliament is to consider the budget proposed by the government, which legislators may amend so long as funding for any additional expenditure is identified. Parliament also considers requests to change overall expenditure once the budget is approved, in view of actual or expected revenue developments.

Parliament, despite the large amount of revenue received through sharing revenue from national taxes or transfers, has no role in approving local government budgets in any of the three countries; they are approved by local councils (with some central government oversight). The size of local budgets is constrained by the size of transfers from central government, revenue-sharing arrangements for national taxes, and limits imposed on their borrowing ability—though these are somewhat ineffective. Local governments do not appear to be bound into an overall fiscal strategy in any of the Baltic countries. In Estonia, local government budgets can include borrowing from domestic or foreign institutions, subject to thresholds related to projected annual revenue. In Lithuania, however, local government budgets must be in balance and municipalities are not allowed to borrow. If they have a financing gap, it must be filled by transfers from the state budget. In Latvia, local governments can only borrow from the treasury and for investment projects that meet certain criteria.

Official definitions of revenue and financing in all three countries are not fully in accordance with international standards. For example, as noted above, the drawdown of financial balances is viewed as a source of revenue rather than as financing. Nevertheless, budget classifications are moving toward standards and practices accepted in countries of the Organization for Economic Cooperation and Development (OECD).[6]

---

[4]See, for example, Alesina and Perotti (1996) and Miles-Ferretti (1996).

[5]Notwithstanding the different national views of the "budget," IMF staff analyses consolidate general government operations, which cover central and local governments plus national extrabudgetary funds.

[6]Privatization receipts are not treated identically in each country and, in particular, are not necessarily part of the official budget. Neither is the treatment of such receipts handled consistently by industrial countries, where they may variously appear as revenue or as a financing item. In Estonia, the bulk of privatization receipts does not feature in the official budget but is handled by an off-budget fund that uses privatization proceeds mainly to defray privatization-related expenses; some small share of privatization receipts is transferred to the Social Insurance Fund. Along with part of the fiscal surpluses generated in Estonia as of 1997, a portion of the privatization receipts is also to be channeled to the Stabilization Reserve Fund, which was established in late 1997. In Latvia and Lithuania, the official budgets consider such receipts to be revenue, while IMF staff analyses usually treat privatization proceeds as financing.

In addition, the official budgets have no consistent treatment of foreign financing. In Estonia, foreign loans are not part of the approved state budget; however, they are on-lent to municipalities or enterprises, or used directly by central government institutions. In Latvia, domestic and foreign loans are part of the official budget and treated in the same way. In Lithuania, while foreign loans are not part of state budget financing, some are used for direct lending to enterprises, and others for direct government expenditure.

The national borrowing strategy is formulated early on in the budget preparation in Lithuania. It also (though more indirectly) forms part of budget formulation in Estonia, at least in determining how much domestic revenue will go to cover investment projects. In Latvia, overall borrowing needs are considered explicitly in preparing the budget.

Purpose of the Budget

In general, the budget should enshrine the important elements of fiscal policy; it may be used for several purposes, notably to facilitate macroeconomic stabilization or to further certain redistributive objectives. Its preparation should provide ample opportunity for the government to delineate its fiscal priorities, and provide a well-ordered system—through careful review of existing programs and the introduction of new programs—for managing government activities. The effectiveness of the budget will also depend on commitment both to the underlying policy package and the manner of fiscal management. In most countries, the budget process is also a tool for political negotiation.

Given these general arguments, the reality in the Baltics so far appears to be that the "state" budget has mainly amounted to an extensive listing of central government or ministerial spending, or both, for which it is believed revenue can be found. In other words, few priorities, if any, have really been identified during the preparation. Consequently, in its execution, the approved budget merely constrains ministerial operations in overall allocation and in categorical allocation.

One area of possible reform therefore is for the Baltic countries to begin to use their budget processes as a means of addressing some of the difficult choices that the transition poses. This means imposing realism and setting priorities about expenditure and funding.

Form of Budget Execution

The manner of budget execution is now changing rapidly in the Baltic countries with the recent introduction of state treasuries, which have provided a significant amount of control over central government expenditure.[7] Previously, there was in general no central control by a "treasury." Instead, each ministry had its own account from which it disbursed its allocated revenue, and the ministry of finance was not fully aware of the financial position of ministries and other spending units. Although monthly reports of budget execution were made, they did not provide a reliable control tool or means of assessing fiscal developments.

Governments' banking arrangements have also undergone significant changes from the days of central planning when government financial operations were conducted through the Gosbank, a practice that persisted with the fledgling central banks during the initial period of transition. Currency board arrangements in Estonia and Lithuania mean that their central banks do not perform the fiscal agent function for budget operations, although they cooperate with the ministry of finance and have oversight of the impact of government operations on the banking system.[8] In Estonia, the treasury operates through several commercial banks. In Lithuania, the State Commercial Bank is the fiscal agent, and in Latvia, it is the central bank. In all cases, the form of banking arrangements has had little detrimental effect on the conduct of government financial operations.

Main Weaknesses of Current Arrangements

Despite the progress that the Baltic countries have made in strengthening budget procedures and enhancing transparency in government finance, there are a number of areas where weaknesses remain.

Adherence to Fiscal Policy Objectives

It has been well stated that a government must give a clear statement of its intentions—its macro-fiscal targets in particular—if there is to be transparency and accountability in government operations (see Garamfalvi and Allan). These targets may be set either in the annual budget or in a medium-term financial plan. For several years, each Baltic country has had an IMF-supported economic program, which provided a broad economic policy framework and specific annual fiscal targets. How-

---

[7]Each of the Baltic countries now has a state treasury, whose functions continue to be broadened to cover at least all central government and, in some cases, national extrabudgetary fund operations. Latvia established central and regional treasury units in 1993; Estonia did likewise from April 1996; and Lithuania began to phase in its treasury operations from June 1996.

[8]In Estonia, this situation changed in late 1997, as the Bank of Estonia was used as the government's agent for the operation of the newly created Stabilization Reserve Fund.

ever, notwithstanding such programs, an inability to mobilize the required political consensus in favor of the "real" fiscal targets (both within the government and parliament) during the budget approval process, partly because of fragmentary political alliances, has made adherence to fiscal policy objectives difficult. There are signs that significant positive changes toward achieving this consensus have been taking place. Given the primacy accorded to fiscal policy within the economic policy arsenal used by the Baltic countries and the limited flexibility of other policy instruments, slippages (actual and perceived) in the fiscal area can be critical.

Lack of Comprehensiveness

Only recently have the authorities in the Baltics fully appreciated the need to consider general government operations. The focus on a narrow institutional coverage of government, together with the lack of a policy framework, can severely limit the assessment of problems and discussion of policy options. The limitation may pose greater problems as structural deficits in social funds place strains on governments' room for maneuver. It is impractical (and not necessarily desirable) for the central government to have full control over local government operations, but there is a need to ensure that all government institutions operate within a common policy framework and to place tighter constraints on local government operations (at least in Estonia). In short, the government and parliament need to show a keener awareness of how municipalities can derail overall fiscal targets.

In discussions about fiscal operations, there is still some confusion over deficit concepts and a narrow view taken of relevant revenue, expenditure, and financing, which stems in part from differences between national and international definitions of these variables. Disagreement over the financial coverage of fiscal operations affects the nature of the dialogue both between the authorities and international agencies such as the IMF, as well as the internal debate that is conducted in parliament or other public forums, and has hampered assessment of the macroeconomic impact of fiscal operations.

Lack of Auditing

Each Baltic country has a legal requirement for the government to present an annual report to parliament on budget execution. This is consistent with the traditional basis of reporting to parliament, in particular its emphasis on compliance with parliamentary authority to spend and transparency in handling public money. However, in the process of creating new fiscal institutions, the Baltics have good opportunities

to move away from these past practices, and could consider offering some critical assessment of the worth of government operations and their "value for money"; this would be a move in the direction of "better" practices and could be seen as enhancing the whole process of governance.[9]

Lack of Coherence and Realism

The underlying budget outlook is often unrealistic as reflected in revenue and expenditure projections that at times merely extrapolate past trends, and may therefore institutionalize practices rather than promote any reevaluation of operations. For example, in Estonia, revenue targets in the budget, based each time on figures that are not up to date, have been lower than actual revenues for several years in a row, partly because the underlying data have not fully reflected the strong pickup in economic growth. This inertia is partly due to a lack of analytical capabilities to develop good revenue forecasts and political will to spell out policy priorities and dispense with less worthy programs.

Important Reforms for the Future

As noted above, substantial reforms that will involve overlapping legislative, institutional, and operational changes are still needed in the Baltic countries. These are outlined below.

Budget exercises should be used as an opportunity for governments to forge a consensus for short- and medium-term priorities in their economic policies and, in the process, encourage efficient use of budget resources. Establishing such priorities could involve development of an early "annual government economic policy statement." The statement could be a means of outlining the main public sector activities and pointing to areas where operations could be phased out or eliminated. It could then form the basis for discussion of fiscal policy and prospects at various levels of government. The discussion should provide ample opportunity for consultation with "cabinet" ministers, local government representatives, and possibly representatives of major segments of the private sector and labor unions. At the end of the process, the budget proposal should reflect clear identification (and acceptance) of priority programs and operations. It is notable that the Estonian government produced such a statement for the first time in 1997 as a prelude to discussions for the

---

[9]See Garamfalvi and Allan (1996), who argue that the recent growing complexity of the role and scope of government activities has created a need for treasuries to enhance transparency by providing better information on the macroeconomic impact of government and value for money from public activities.

1998 budget. Latvia intends to introduce two-year budgets, starting in 1998–99, to strengthen the medium-term focus of fiscal policy, and Lithuania is likewise engaged in the preparation of a medium-term fiscal program, the first version of which was discussed in the context of the 1998 budget preparations.

Government institutions should be bound to an overall macroeconomic and fiscal framework. Part of this binding process will be based on (1) the obligation of ministries to work within the macroeconomic guidelines provided by the ministry of finance; and (2) development of controls such as limits on general government borrowing that are made binding by requiring that the ministry of finance give its prior approval to borrowing proposals (and that transgressions be met with effective penalties, for example, the risk of losing transfers from the central government, or the real risk of bankruptcy if there is default).[10] Part of this process will be achieved less directly. In setting up the framework, it is important that the ministry of finance establish units responsible for developing a macroeconomic framework for the budget projections. Fledgling units of this kind have now been established in each country, but need to feature more prominently in the development of policy.

Budget laws should be changed to incorporate (1) a broader definition of government; (2) internationally accepted definitions of revenue and financing; and (3) comprehensive coverage of fiscal operations. These elements would then ensure that budgets cover (1) all sources of revenue (tax and nontax); (2) all expenditure, current and capital, whether associated with wholly domestically funded or foreign funded operations, plus any government lending operations; and (3) all forms of domestic and foreign financing.

The authorities should be encouraged to move permanently away from using cash control and sequestration as a method of expenditure management in place of setting priorities properly within the budget.[11] Sequestration and cash limits clearly have relevance in the very short term, especially when opportunities to borrow are limited. However, such practices are not adequate substitutes for proper identification of medium-term budgetary priorities and adequate funding for the resultant programs.

The authorities should begin a review of revenue sharing arrangements and assess the need to reform

local government finance. Such a review is already under way in Lithuania; and a World Bank study of Estonia has made several proposals to address these issues.[12]

There should be fuller auditing and evaluation of government operations. Nonpartisan governmental commissions already exist to perform audits of fiscal operations. But these are meant to focus on whether budget appropriations have been used as intended, that is, on accounting for expenditure rather than on valuating the worthiness of spending. Such commissions could serve a useful function if they were redirected toward evaluations, and could thus help in better identifying appropriate priorities for expenditure.

Fiscal Revenue Mobilization

A high degree of fiscal revenue mobilization may be necessary if the Baltic countries are to achieve a western European standard of living and level of services. Given the proximity of the Baltics to Scandinavia, they may wish to emulate the latter countries' fiscal policies, which have necessitated ratios of fiscal revenue to GDP in the range of 50 percent to 60 percent. If the Baltics were to follow the example of European countries in general or smaller OECD countries, they would have to mobilize fiscal revenue in the range of 45 percent of GDP.[13] However, such levels of revenue mobilization tend to be high for countries at income levels similar to the Baltics.

Within the Soviet system, the Baltic countries had attained high levels of fiscal revenue mobilization during the decade prior to the start of transition. In the early years of transition, the Baltics have broadly maintained high levels of fiscal revenue relative to GDP compared with Russia and other countries of the CIS.[14] In the process, there has been some slight shift in the structure of revenue in the Baltics since 1993 (Table 4.1). Direct taxes (mainly on corporate and personal income, and on payrolls) have stabilized or declined in the three countries. There has been a tendency for indirect taxes (mainly VAT and excise taxes) to gain in importance. The significance of the corporate income tax has plummeted, while the personal income and payroll taxes have not declined as dramatically. With these changes, the struc-

---

[10]Such an approach has been adopted in Latvia and Estonia in setting conditions for local government borrowing.

[11]Even with the development of treasuries, there continues to be a tendency to control expenditure by cash limits and sequestration.

[12]See World Bank (1995).

[13]See IMF (1996a), Chapter III.

[14]Lithuania experienced an early collapse of revenues that reflected a significant decline in the tax base for corporate income because profits declined sharply and exemptions were generous. VAT and exmmmcise tax income also fell markedly owing to considerable problems in tax collection and evasion.

Table 4.1. Fiscal Revenues
(Percent of GDP)

	1991	1992	1993	1994	1995	1996	1997
Total revenue							
Estonia	41.0	34.6	38.5	41.3	39.9	39.0	38.9
Latvia	37.4	28.2	36.4	36.5	35.5	36.8	39.9
Lithuania	...	32.0	30.2	32.6	32.3	29.6	32.7
Direct taxes[1]							
Estonia	24.6	22.3	24.6	24.6	23.8	22.7	22.1
Latvia	21.5	17.8	23.2	19.7	18.7	18.5	19.3
Lithuania	...	18.7	17.7	19.3	18.4	17.4	18.9
Indirect taxes[2]							
Estonia	13.4	9.4	11.2	13.6	13.0	13.4	13.9
Latvia	10.1	6.5	8.8	11.2	11.8	13.4	13.5
Lithuania	...	11.0	9.3	11.0	12.4	10.6	12.5

Sources: Country authorities; and IMF staff estimates.

[1]Income, payroll, and land taxes.

[2]Value-added taxes, excises, and taxes on international trade.

ture of revenue has become closer to that of western economies.

How Were High Levels of Revenue Sustained During Early Transition Years?

Early in the transition, the Baltic countries introduced comprehensive tax reforms, adopted market-style tax regimes, and subsequently sought to keep their tax systems simple. Estonia initiated its tax reform in 1991 with the introduction of a new social tax on employers, a progressive personal income tax (PIT), and a broad-based western style VAT (at an initial unified rate of 10 percent), which replaced taxes on turnover and mark-up margins. Additional tax reforms in 1992 involved the introduction of a new medical insurance tax, an increase in the unified VAT rate to 18 percent, and consolidation of the corporate income tax (CIT) rates into a single rate (35 percent). New VAT and income tax laws in 1994 eliminated exemptions and provisions for special treatment (e.g., the removal of investment incentives); reduced and simplified rates further (e.g., introduced a single PIT rate of 26 percent); and generally adopted market principles and practices in line with western European countries. Estonia has no import duties (except on furs and water pleasure craft), and only a few duties on exports of items of cultural value.

Lithuania began to replace its Soviet tax laws as of mid-1990. A simplified VAT (replacing the general

excise tax) was introduced in December 1991—initially at a rate of 20 percent, which was quickly changed to 15 percent, and then raised to 18 percent in July 1992; it became a fully fledged VAT in 1994. Specific excise taxes were also developed and, in due course, were changed to ad valorem taxes—on alcohol from September 1992, and on petroleum products from March 1993. All excises now have ad valorem rates, ranging from 10 percent to 50 percent. The operation of the PIT and CIT has been relatively complex, with numerous rates and preferential treatment (e.g., for joint ventures and enterprises that reinvest profits). But there have been attempts to simplify the laws; amended draft laws on the PIT and CIT have been submitted to parliament and redrafted several times in the past two to three years, including in 1997. The latest draft incorporates a unified rate. There are import tariffs, which are applied using a three-tier system dependent on country of origin, and which embody a wide mixture of rates for different products as well as preferential treatment for certain countries.

Latvia set up a new tax system in January 1991. At the beginning of 1992, the authorities introduced a VAT with a 10 percent standard rate (and various surcharges) to replace the turnover tax. A new excise tax law was adopted in October 1992. The income tax system was not reformed until early 1995, when a unified, standard rate of 25 percent was introduced. A new set of excise tax rates was implemented in 1996—on gasoline, diesel, and alcohol—which boosted revenue significantly. Latvia levies both import and export duties, the former geared more toward protection of agriculture, the latter geared toward minerals, forestry products, and art. The rate structure of such duties is relatively simple.

Now all Baltic states have average tax rates that are broadly consistent with the average in the EU and their industrial European neighbors (e.g., a VAT rate of 18 percent in all three countries; income tax rates of about 25 percent (in Latvia and Estonia)). Lithuania is considering a uniform income tax rate.[15] The structure of revenue is also now closer to the OECD average.

Tax reforms in the Baltics have tended to remove many exemptions and forms of special treatment. Agriculture (small farmers) remains the one sector that regularly receives exceptional treatment. There are also many instances where groups of ailing enterprises or specific commodities are given preferential treatment, for example, income or VAT exemptions for agricultural enterprises, and tax exemptions for food and some fuel. In Latvia, these are in addition to high external tariffs. Lithuania eliminated the VAT exemptions with the 1997 budget.

Tax collection has been bolstered by mandatory use of tax withholding for income taxes and the fact that there is little need for individuals to complete tax returns. The role of banks in tax collection has been relatively limited.

In all three countries, the process of substantial reorganization of tax administration has begun, with the objective of developing services that are related to tax types rather than taxpayers. Estonia established an aggressive approach to nonpayment of taxes and resolution of payment arrears, including attempts to use the legal system, though with mixed success and some opposition from the courts, which were concerned with protecting debtors. Consequently, the stock of tax arrears is not a major problem, with total tax arrears on the order of 3–4 percent of GDP. In addition, mechanisms for working out arrangements to settle overdue tax liabilities have been instituted (or in some instances, the liabilities have been forgiven as part of privatization). However, at some 10 percent of GDP, tax arrears are a greater problem in Latvia, notably in relation to particular sectors (such as energy enterprises). While arrears to the central government in Lithuania are not large (around 2 percent of GDP), periodic tax amnesties have played a role.

Each country has developed expertise in tax administration through use of technical assistance from the IMF and extensive training provided by other national tax agencies. In addition, the Baltic tax authorities have used limited amounts of collaboration and international information sharing to establish a firmer base for their knowledge of taxpayers' taxable income and activities (e.g., in association with Scandinavian countries and INTERPOL).

Overall, the Baltic countries have quickly developed good tax systems in terms of tax structure and rates. Their bigger problem at present is in the administration of taxes, in particular to ensure full collection. This reflects at its simplest the effect of exemptions, but also greater sophistication in finding ways to avoid taxes, and more intractable problems of tax evasion that result from fraud and corruption.

What Are the Immediate and Medium-Term Problems?

The burden of payroll tax rates is high by international standards (currently 31 percent in Lithuania; 33 percent in Estonia; and 37 percent in Latvia but scheduled to decline gradually to 33 percent by 2001). Such high tax rates (borne almost exclusively by employers in the first instance) create incentives to distort the labor market through alternative or irregular forms of employment and compensation.

Evasion and avoidance remain widespread. Notwithstanding progress in some areas (e.g., Lithuania's impressive efforts in 1997 in addressing tax administration deficiencies), there is a risk that such practices could become entrenched. Incentives to engage in evasive activities need to be removed and official tolerance of this behavior likewise should be reduced. The governance problems that emerge when public sector institutions and top officials are the culprits must be addressed promptly. It is important that tax treatment be even handed and that particular groups not receive favorable treatment when they are guilty of evasion. Penalties need to be effective, visible, and easy to implement.

Opposition from vested interests to the introduction of new or wider taxation or to changes in expenditure priorities has been strong. It has come in particular from (1) groups of enterprises (e.g., ailing state-owned operations and successful enterprises wishing to see their foreign earnings remain untaxed); (2) certain economic sectors (e.g., agriculture); and (3) politicians or political groups (who do not appear to be concerned about conflicts of interest, e.g., in Estonia, the many national politicians who are also local government politicians) that benefit unduly from existing fiscal arrangements. Associated with this is the considerable political fear of the inflationary impact of tax changes, which may induce delays in making necessary changes.

---

[15]At present, Lithuania's corporate income tax rate is 29 percent, and the peronal income tax rate is 33 percent.

How Can High Levels of Revenue Mobilization Be Sustained?

It is necessary to build on elements of good design (e.g., simple tax systems) and carry out stricter enforcement (e.g., nontolerance of blatant tax evasion) as indicated in the following recommendations.

- Further improve tax administration, in particular, coordination between tax collection agencies (i.e., national tax boards and customs administrations) so that there will be consistent data on taxpayers, and a regular and comprehensive exchange of information. In Estonia, there could also be better coordination of taxes collected from the same or similar revenue bases (i.e., income taxes and payroll taxes, responsibility for which is separated between the National Tax Board (NTB) and the Ministry of Social Affairs, respectively; only the former has the legal right to pursue delinquent payers). Moreover, there is scope for better coordination on issues of goods valuation, where substantial VAT or excise tax revenue may leak away through the acceptance of bogus valuations.
- Strengthen cooperation between the tax authorities and banking system in an effort to assess the reliability of income declarations, while protecting the confidentiality of banking transactions.
- Improve coordination between the tax authorities and the legal system. In Estonia, for example, the aggressive approach of the NTB has been thwarted by opposition in the courts, where judges have made it difficult to pursue even flagrant cases of tax evasion. Lack of capacity and expertise in commercial courts may also be an important problem.
- Increase the effectiveness of taxes by better covering the emerging private sector, perhaps with the use of tax payer identification numbers and more aggressive monitoring of enterprise registration. In addition, the buoyancy of taxes could be improved by making excises ad valorem rather than specific. All three countries have experienced significant problems in identifying new enterprises and taxable activities. Furthermore, the relatively open borders make it difficult to counteract the high degree of smuggling that apparently exists. There is some evidence that technical assistance to overcome some of these customs-related problems, in particular by the British Crown Agents (in Latvia and Estonia), can be effective.
- Widen the tax net, notably to better cover energy products (e.g., gasoline) and (all) forms of unearned income. Extending taxes on land and property would also be desirable, but must perhaps await further progress in land privatization.

In addition, the authorities should extend taxes to cover new activities to prevent the creation of loopholes for tax avoidance or evasion.

- Keep taxes on the use of natural resources and creation of pollution up to date to encourage efficient use of natural resources and accumulate funding for environmental protection measures.
- Ensure that taxes are not disguised trade barriers by, among other things, equalizing taxes on domestic and foreign goods, simplifying forms, and providing information to taxpayers.
- Reduce the burden of compliance on taxpayers by indexing or periodically changing thresholds (this may be important for new, small enterprises in the context of the VAT).[16]
- Improve compliance through operational changes, for example, use of cash registers and invoices to provide audit trails for excises and the VAT, development of large tax payer units, and special tax arrears collection units.
- Reduce the use of revenue sharing and improve local governments' own tax base. The desirability of such measures must be tempered by the need for a proper evaluation of government functions, and appropriate expenditure assignment and reorganization of local government and intergovernmental fiscal relations. Internationally, local governments tend to function better when they have adequate local taxes to cover local services. In this regard, property and land taxes as well as some element of local income or sales taxes are appropriate. However, bestowing more financial powers on local government may have implications for macroeconomic and fiscal management in the medium term. Already, Latvia has land and property taxes that accrue wholly to local government. Estonia has only a land tax that previously accrued to both central and local governments, but now goes entirely to municipalities. A range of minor local taxes (in terms of their revenue potential) is now available to municipalities in Estonia.
- Improve tax analysis to better assess the impact of policy options. This is already beginning to be done in Lithuania through the establishment of a macroeconomic policy department at the Ministry of Finance, the aim of which is to evaluate the revenue implications of alternative tax policy scenarios and, more generally, to assess the macroeconomic implications of a particular budgetary stance.

---

[16]Ironically, in Estonia, many enterprises chose not to deregister for the VAT when the threshold was raised, as such registration bestowed on them certain advantages such as credibility and prominence in the market place.

Expenditure Management and Rationalization

While the authorities in the Baltic states have made considerable progress in reforming revenues, they have made few attempts at fundamentally changing the level or structure of expenditures. This section examines some of the key issues that the Baltic countries face in expenditure management.

Recent Developments and Policy Issues

The size of government in the Baltics, with government expenditure representing about 40 percent of GDP in Estonia, 38 percent in Latvia, and somewhat less in Lithuania, 34 percent, is higher than in countries at similar income levels, and almost as high as in lower income members of the EU (Table 4.2).[17] In this regard, the Baltic countries seem to have bucked one trend prevalent in the CIS during the transition, that is, a considerable decline in the level of expenditure. In all countries, general government expenditures as a share of GDP actually increased between 1992 and 1996, although in Lithuania the increase was smaller in magnitude.

Expenditure patterns in the Baltics—with some variation among the three states—have mirrored those in the CIS in several respects. First, spending in Latvia in particular has tended to favor current over capital outlays, which have fallen to low levels (1–2 percent of GDP). By contrast, public investment has been maintained at respectable levels in Estonia (4–5 percent of GDP) and Lithuania (3–4 percent of GDP). Second, outlays on the social safety net (comprising pensions, family allowances, unemployment compensation, and other transfers to households) have been high in Estonia and Lithuania (averaging 11 percent and 10 percent of GDP, respectively, in 1993–96) and especially in Latvia (rising from 14 percent of GDP in 1993 to 16 percent in 1994–96). Some of these expenditures have been desirable, for example, energy and housing allowances replacing subsidies, and social assistance and unemployment benefits going to vulnerable households hit by income declines. But rising pension payments are a key factor behind high social, and total, spending. Third, expenditure on health and education continues to absorb large amounts of resources, reflecting a system inherited from the planned economy that is characterized by excessive staffing and physical capacity, misdirected spending, and declining at-

tainment indicators. During the period 1992–95 in Estonia and Latvia, spending on health and education rose in relation to GDP, and in addition, real spending on these two sectors appears to have increased substantially.[18]

A notable feature of general government expenditures in the Baltics is the relatively large wage bill. At about 10 percent of GDP, the wage bill in those three countries compares with wages and salaries equivalent to 5 percent of GDP in the CIS, and 12 percent of GDP for smaller and European OECD countries. Taking the case of Estonia, the size of the wage bill mainly reflects a large public service, which represents about 18 percent of the labor force and 8 percent of the population, levels that prevail in the OECD (Table 4.3). In addition, public sector wages have increased as a share of the national average wage level, that is, roughly from 80 percent in 1993 to 95 percent in 1996.[19]

Key Policy Choices

The Baltic countries are reaching the stage where they have to address basic questions about overall expenditure patterns and priorities. Simply increasing expenditure is not a credible option for several reasons: (1) there are limits to revenue mobilization, and as noted above, revenues in the Baltics are already high; (2) there is every indication that these states will continue to follow a cautious borrowing policy; and (3) there is a need to contain the size of government in line with the workings of a market economy. This section does not tackle the question of the appropriate level of expenditures (which encompasses many different cultural and economic factors), but with reform, it may well decline in all countries.[20]

The focus of reforms must be on overhauling budget institutions and procedures (see Section II) and restructuring expenditure programs, especially to improve the cost effectiveness of current operations and to provide for infrastructural investment, which is critical to economic growth. In reviewing their expenditure priorities, the authorities will face myriad decisions, for example, on the split between current and capital spending, and between wage and nonwage current spending; the scale and nature of social

---

[17]These numbers for the Baltics refer to 1996. The ratio of expenditure to GDP in 1994 stood at an average of 20 percent in Chile, Colombia, Korea, Thailand, and Turkey. World Bank (1996), p. 112.

[18]Health care spending in Latvia grew by more than 20 percent in real terms in 1995, with almost all of the increase coming from spending on primary health care.

[19]World Bank (1997).

[20]A substantial reduction in expenditures as a share of GDP could take time, underscoring the importance of maintaining a strong revenue performance. Moreover, revenues will be needed to help finance pension reform.

Table 4.2. General Government Expenditures in the Baltics and Selected EU Countries
(Percent of GDP)

	1991	1992	1993	1994	1995	1996
Estonia						
Total expenditure and net lending	35.7	34.8	39.1	40.1	41.2	40.6
Total expenditure	35.7	33.7	36.9	38.5	40.8	40.5
Current	31.9	32.3	34.1	34.3	36.1	35.6
Goods and services	17.4	22.1	21.5	22.0	24.3	23.8
Wages and salaries[1]	4.5	7.8	7.1	10.6	10.3	9.4
Transfers to households[2]	11.7	8.3	10.2	10.4	10.8	11.2
Of which: Pensions	2.9	5.5	6.4	6.5	7.0	7.6
Interest payments	—	—	0.1	0.3	0.4	0.3
Capital	3.8	1.4	2.8	4.1	4.6	4.9
Net lending	—	1.1	2.2	1.6	0.4	0.1
Memorandum item						
Health and education	...	...	10.0	12.4	12.3	...
Latvia						
Total expenditure and net lending	31.1	30.0	35.7	40.5	38.8	38.2
Total expenditure	31.1	28.2	35.3	38.2	38.2	38.0
Current	28.0	26.7	33.7	37.1	37.3	36.2
Wages and salaries	4.6	6.2	7.7	8.7	10.2	8.7
Transfers to households[2]	11.4	9.6	14.2	16.3	16.0	16.2
Of which: Pensions	...	6.2	9.6	9.8	9.6	10.2
Interest payments	—	0.1	0.9	0.6	1.2	1.3
Capital	3.0	1.5	1.2	1.1	0.9	1.7
Net lending	—	0.8	0.4	2.3	0.6	0.2
Memorandum item						
Health and education	...	...	10.1	10.2	10.5	9.9
Lithuania						
Total expenditure and net lending	...	30.2	35.4	37.4	36.8	34.1
Total expenditure	...	29.8	30.1	33.8	34.9	32.1
Current	...	27.3	26.0	31.0	29.9	29.4
Wages and salaries	...	...	5.9	8.7	9.2	9.6
Transfers to households[2]	...	6.2	9.6	10.8	9.9	9.9
Of which: Pensions	...	5.5	4.7	6.3	6.2	6.1
Subsidies to enterprises	...	2.0	1.4	1.7	1.1	1.3
Interest payments	...	—	—	0.1	0.4	0.9
Capital	...	2.5	3.4	3.9	3.8	2.7
Net lending	...	0.4	5.4	3.6	1.9	2.0
Memorandum item						
Health and education	...	...	...	...	9.4	8.9
Selected EU countries						
Total expenditure and net lending						
Greece	51.1	52.4	55.3	55.0	53.2	51.2
Ireland	40.5	41.1	40.9	41.3	44.6	44.6
Portugal	46.5	46.5	47.5	45.8	46.3	47.3
Spain	45.3	46.3	49.5	48.0	47.3	45.4

Sources: Country statistical authorities; and IMF staff estimates.

[1]A portion of wages and salaries is classified under purchases of goods and services.

[2]Comprising pensions, family allowances, unemployment compensation, and other transfers to households.

protection; and the expenditure responsibilities of the central and local governments. In addition, they will undoubtedly continue to face great pressure to support nonfinancial public enterprises that are struggling, an important issue in the energy sector in Latvia and Lithuania, and to protect the program of

Table 4.3. General Government Wage Bill and Employment in the Baltics and Selected European Countries

General Government Wage Bill[1]	As Percent of GDP	As Percent of Total Expenditure
Estonia[2]	9.4	23.0
Latvia	8.7	23.0
Lithuania	9.6	29.8
Belgium	10.1	17.8
Germany	8.1	14.8
Spain	9.9	19.6
United Kingdom	10.4	18.6

General Government Employment, 1995	As Percent of Population	As Percent of Total Employment
Estonia	8.0	18.0
Latvia	8.3	17.7
Lithuania	8.4	18.8
Denmark	13.4	26.5
France	7.7	19.6
Germany	4.9	10.4
Sweden	18.1	34.9
OECD average	8.1	18.4

Sources: IMF staff estimates; and World Bank (1997).
[1]1996 data for the Baltic countries, and 1992 data for European countries.
[2]Estimate.

various extrabudgetary funds. But there is little, if anything, to gain from inaction ("postponing unpopularity"), including the use of underbudgeting and sequestration to postpone curbing expenditure (see Cheasty and Davis, 1996).

Pension Systems

This section limits itself to two areas that will have a significant influence on future trends in expenditures, that is, social benefits, notably pensions, because these have placed a growing burden on public finances in the Baltics, and intergovernmental fiscal relations, because experience in Estonia in particular has shown that local government spending can quickly become a serious problem.

Current Status

As in many other transition economies, the pension funds in Estonia and Lithuania still operate on a pay-as-you-go (PAYG) basis. Latvia adopted a major pension reform in late 1995, but shares a number of the following problems with the other Baltic states:

(1) High old age and child dependency ratios. The ratio of pensioners to contributors to the social insurance system has reached 0.5 in Estonia (1996) and 0.87 in Latvia (end-1995), that is, one pensioner is supported by only two contributors in Estonia and just over one contributor in Latvia.[21]

(2) High statutory tax rates, notably for the payroll tax, which create incentives for employers to shift components of labor compensation out of the wage fund—the very basis for the payroll tax.[22]

---

[21]These ratios are comparable with or higher than those in a number of European countries, for example, Austria (0.59), Spain (0.46), Sweden (0.37), and Switzerland (0.42). Data for European countries refer to 1993.

[22]Social Security and total payroll tax rates are, respectively, 20 percent and 33 percent in Estonia, and 22.5 percent and 30 percent in Lithuania; the social security tax rate stands at 37 percent in Latvia. While the total payroll tax rates in the Baltics are lower than those in such countries as France, Italy, and the Netherlands (about 55 percent), they are higher or comparable to those in other western European countries, such as Norway (25 percent), Sweden (32 percent), Ireland (22 percent), and Switzerland (23 percent). Data for European countries refer to 1993.

(3) The increase in unemployment (and underemployment) and the fall in real wages compared with the pretransition era[23] have boosted the number of households in need.

(4) The increasing importance of informal sector activities and private transfers, and the decline in the share of wages and government cash benefits in average household income. This has made it harder for governments to identify the poor.

Against this backdrop, pension systems in the Baltics have carried on as under the old system, typically providing generous benefits: almost universal coverage; special privileges for a broad range of groups (e.g., as in Estonia, individuals entitled to early retirement such as parents of disabled children, dwarfs, participants in the Chernobyl rescue operation, and those illegally detained; or for whom noncontributing periods count toward length of service, such as members of the armed forces and of artistic and professional unions); and an early retirement age.[24] The result is that the pension funds are in financial trouble. In Estonia, after accumulating reserves for three years in a row, the Social Insurance Fund drew down reserves in 1996 to finance a growing deficit on its operations.[25] In Latvia, the Social Insurance Fund also ran a deficit in 1996. Lithuania introduced a restructured social security scheme in 1994, and the Social Insurance Fund was able to at least maintain balance in 1995 and 1996, but experienced some problems in early 1997 linked to increases in pensions and other benefits.

The pension funds in Estonia and Lithuania—the new Latvian system is discussed below—provide defined benefits that depend on workers' earnings rather than on contributions and that are financed by payroll taxes on a PAYG basis. This system results in a wide array of problems, that is, high payroll tax rates; misallocation of public resources (directed to pensions rather than education, and so forth); a lost opportunity to increase long-term saving; failure to redistribute resources to low income groups; and unintended intergenerational transfers. As a consequence, existing systems have not always protected the elderly and will not protect those who will be old in the near future.

In the absence of major policy initiatives, the near-term prospects for these funds, as in other transition economies, are bleak. Given demographic trends, the current PAYG systems cannot continue to provide the generous benefits common under central planning. In fact, they are not fiscally sustainable. There appears to be no scope for raising payroll taxes further without a substantial negative impact on wages or labor demand. And at present, central government budgets cannot be expected to fill the gap between pension fund obligations and revenues. Without reform, pensioners and the unemployed will bear the brunt of the income decline.

Reform Options

The reform of social protection needs to take place within a broad policy framework. First, it requires the establishment of clear priorities among budgetary expenditures and improvements in domestic resource mobilization. For example, it may be less distortive to cut government expenditure or even to increase consumption taxes than to raise payroll taxes to contain a pension-related deterioration in fiscal balances. Second, it must take into account the growing importance of informal activity. Third, it entails better targeting of existing benefits and the use of the resultant savings to shield the truly vulnerable as well as greater reliance on self-targeting (though this could increase the stigma for beneficiaries). In this regard, policymakers need additional information to determine who are the needy and underemployed; who is participating in the informal sector; the number of social benefit recipients; and the number of enterprises obliged to pay payroll taxes. Finally, it must be based on careful examination and calculations of the costs of different pension promises and reform options, and their impact on the overall fiscal position.[26]

Without detailed studies of the pension systems in the Baltics, it is difficult to be prescriptive beyond stating that all three Baltic states should strengthen their existing systems and also move toward some form of funded scheme to supplement current arrangements. It may be useful to sketch the main steps and their sequencing that have come out of international experience, as well as the three broad models of reform that have emerged (including the Latvian concept).

A first step: parametric reform. This step would consist of implementing measures to change the parameters of the existing pension system. Given that the contribution rates (payroll taxes) are high, the focus is on expenditure-reducing measures such as

---

[23]See World Bank (1996), Table 4.3, which indicates that real wages in Estonia and Latvia in 1994 were roughly 50 percent and 60 percent of the level prevailing in 1989.

[24]Estonia has begun to increase the retirement age by six months every year until it reaches 65 years for both men and women. Lithuania has announced the intention to proceed along the same path.

[25]In 1997, this fund posted a small surplus owing to a large increase in revenues as the economy grew very rapidly.

---

[26]Estonia initiated such a study in March 1997.

increasing the statutory retirement age to slow down the growth in the number of beneficiaries and tightening the eligibility criteria for early retirement and disability pensions (and in the process removing most special privileges). Additional measures would aim at lowering the level of per capita benefits by modifying either the mechanism determining increases in the benefits of existing pensioners (e.g., curbing the power of parliament in Estonia to determine pension increases) or the initial benefit for new pensioners (e.g., extending the period of a worker's earning history used to establish the assessed income in determining the initial pension).

A second step: systemic reform. This step would involve replacing the defined-benefit approach with a defined-contribution system. Such a move would be based on the dual premise that the financing mechanism of a PAYG system lies at the root of the financial imbalances and that the development of financial reserves (through partial or full funding) would reduce the need for unsustainable increases in payroll or contribution rates. Phased in over a longer period, these measures would be aimed at putting in place:

(1) A first-tier mandatory pension scheme that provides a fixed minimum social pension for all those eligible (financed from general revenues). It would resemble existing pension plans but focus on the redistribution of resources.

(2) A second PAYG tier offering earnings-related benefits with strict caps. This scheme, with its emphasis on saving, would differ significantly from the current systems in Estonia and Lithuania, and link benefits actuarially to contributions (to discourage evasion). It would be made mandatory so as to compensate for individual "short-sightedness." Private management of the funds would promote economic over political considerations and encourage investment diversification.

(3) A fully funded third tier based on individual savings retirement accounts. This voluntary scheme would supplement the first two tiers and provide benefits proportional to the amounts contributed over the individual's working life.

Several countries have adopted variations of the multipillar system; the way in which their reforms were implemented reflects different initial conditions and political economies. There are three basic models:

The Latin American model. Under this approach, pioneered in Chile in 1980, workers are able to choose the investment managers of their own individual accounts. This model is being actively considered in Hungary and Poland but has not been adopted outside Latin America. The countries that adopted this approach started with bloated public pillars and high contribution rates.

The OECD model. Many employer-sponsored pension plans, which existed on a voluntary basis, became the foundation for a mandatory second pillar; a combination of employer and union trustees choose the investment manager. At the outset, these countries had a modest redistributive pillar and a small "implicit pension debt"; they could therefore retain the first pillar and add a second pillar.

The partial European model. This approach rests on notional-defined contribution plans or large tax incentives for voluntary funded plans. Countries with large public pillars and implicit pension debt are having great difficulty in making the transition to a scheme with both a partially funded and a mandatory private pillar—partly because of financing problems, partly because of political interests. The notional account system was pioneered (though not yet adopted) by Sweden.

Latvia, the only Baltic state to have implemented a far-reaching pension reform, provides a concrete example of a "notional-defined contribution" pension system.[27] The Latvian approach directly links benefits to individual contributions and the retirement age. It also provides for the introduction of funded pension programs, initially as a supplement to the public system. In 1998, contributors will be allowed to allocate a portion of their payroll tax to individual, privately managed accounts. In essence, the approach mimics the contribution-based pension that would be offered in the private sector. The system starts by giving everyone paying the social tax an individual account. As contributions earmarked for the pension system are paid, the account is credited as if it were a savings account. The "capital" in the account earns a rate of return just like a savings account. This rate of return is equal to the growth of the wage base on which contributions are collected (the contribution wage base). At retirement, the pension paid is equal to the total capital in the person's account divided by the expected postretirement life span for all those of that person's age. The pension will be indexed, fully adjusting for price changes. In the new system, there is no mandatory retirement age and no "full pension." The minimum retirement age will be 60 years for most participants, but the system offers strong incentives to work longer.

The government in Lithuania is considering a form of the three-tier option, possibly with a pri-

---

[27]In November 1995, parliament approved legislation to create a new public system for those who retire after 1995; pensions for current pensioners were not affected.

vately funded third tier. Two independent non-government teams are currently preparing drafts for private pension options to be discussed for implementation. The authorities in Estonia have also indicated their intention of moving to a partially funded system and have begun to take steps in this direction.

Financing the Transition.

In moving from a PAYG scheme to a new defined-contribution scheme, benefits to existing pensioners (under the defined-benefit system) would continue to be the responsibility of the government (or the former pension funds). Yet contributions of some (to be determined) component of the labor force would be channeled, not for the financing of these pension outlays, but for investment into some form of pension-related, individually linked savings accounts. Thus, the government would be faced with the obligation of having to meet continuing pension liabilities for what might be a lengthy period, but without the offsetting flow of payroll contributions. The size of the deficits that would emerge would depend on how quickly the funded schemes are introduced. There are two options:

(1) A "sudden" transition, where the switch to a partially funded, defined-contribution system is made at one point in time, and applies to all pensioners and future beneficiaries.

(2) A "gradual" transition, where only new entrants to the labor force become members of a partially funded, defined-contribution scheme (this may take several years depending on survival rates for beneficiaries still subject to the defined-benefit, PAYG system). In view of the large pension liabilities and the early stage of development of the financial system, this option is the more attractive of the two for the Baltics.

The strategies adopted in Latin America have dealt with all the major issues involved in pension reform and may have something to offer Estonia and Lithuania in particular. The principles underlying these strategies are as follows:

- Before the transition, reform the old system by reducing benefits; raise the retirement age and penalties for early retirement; tighten eligibility requirements for disability benefits; and change the method of indexation to prevent unrealistic benefit promises from becoming entrenched.
- Build up a primary surplus in the general treasury that can be used to pay part of the liabilities to existing pensioners (perhaps also use any existing surplus in the social security system or privatization proceeds for this purpose).
- Keep certain workers in the old system (e.g., military personnel).

- Educate the public on the need for and desirability of change.
- Minimize evasion, and modernize tax collection and information systems.

Family Benefits

Current Status

Family benefits in the Baltics comprise sickness, maternity, and universal family benefits, and constitute about 3–4 percent of GDP. Most of these benefits are not means-tested. In Lithuania, for example, this is true of the "categorical" benefits (allowances to single mothers, birth grants and child care allowances, funeral grants and guardians' allowances). The top three income deciles received 25 percent of the cash benefits during 1994. Further progress has been made in targeting social assistance more effectively toward those with clear needs and limited incomes, namely, by introducing (and targeting better) the special social benefit that provides basic income support to those on low incomes and that is tested on the basis of household income per capita.[28] In Estonia, about 40 percent of all benefits accrue to the richest 50 percent of the population. Child benefits, potentially the most progressive assistance, are universal. Moreover, the heavy emphasis on housing assistance and institutional care programs constrains the ability of social assistance offices to respond to the needs of the population. The only social assistance program where poorer counties receive a larger share of per capita cash benefits than better off counties is the income support program; it is means-tested and aims at raising household income levels to a minimum standard but accounts for less than one-third of all social assistance.

Reform Options

Experience so far suggests the following ways of strengthening family benefits in the Baltics:

- Enhance administrative efficiency by simplifying the structure of the numerous family benefits that government ministries and social insurance funds finance, and by consolidating them into a smaller number of benefits whose maximum size is larger.[29]

---

[28]Recent changes reduced the proportion of the population receiving the special social benefit from about 45 percent to 15–18 percent. Most of this reduction was achieved by consolidating the special social benefit payable to pensioners with the pension benefit itself.

[29]In Lithuania, the number of state-provided social assistance benefits to families was reduced from 12 to 8 in 1994.

- Improve monitoring of living standards and its link to policy formulation. Analysis of data from household budget surveys could play a larger role in spending decisions on social cash benefits. At present, decisions are driven almost exclusively by budget considerations. While this supports fiscal discipline, it provides little guidance to benefit targeting. Another important step would be to improve the household surveys themselves.

- Review eligibility less frequently for those benefits of longer duration, but require beneficiaries to advise the ministry if their eligibility or circumstances change.

- Extend the scope of means-testing to target a greater share of social assistance on people with the least resources and, in this way, facilitate larger benefits for those without other income. Two possible approaches are noted here. First, the authorities could choose to improve targeting to families with many children, a proxy for poverty. Accordingly, they could means test child benefits, with the threshold set at a high enough level that only children of the richest 50 percent of households are screened out. Second, the authorities could consider allowing local-level social assistance offices to allocate funds between social assistance programs according to local needs. For example, the funds for social assistance could be inversely related to per capita personal income tax revenues of the local government.

Intergovernmental Fiscal Relations

Intergovernmental fiscal relations have been a major problem in the Baltics, particularly in Estonia where local government autonomy has had the potential to derail fiscal policy. The main problem relates to control over local government borrowing (an issue that could be considered part of the budget process).

Cross-country experience suggests that direct controls over local government borrowing tend to be looser where overall financial discipline is poor, and fiscal and macroeconomic disequilibria have not been addressed (typically in transition and developing economies), or where well-developed and relatively transparent financial systems can rely on the market to discipline subnational government borrowing. This experience (described in Ter-Minassian, 1996) may hold some lessons for the Baltics:

- Greater transparency and dissemination of information on recent and prospective developments in subnational government finances is highly desirable; governments should be en-

couraged to change the legal and institutional framework to promote these objectives.

- Sole reliance on market discipline is unlikely to be appropriate in many circumstances, but may be a useful complement to other controls.

- Rules-based approaches to debt control appear preferable in terms of transparency and certainty. There is a clear macroeconomic rationale for barring all local government borrowing from the central bank; borrowing abroad by subnational government, if not consolidated through the central government, should be strictly limited.

- There is a case, in principle at least, for limiting all borrowing to investment purposes where there are adequate rates of economic and social return.

These guidelines seem to argue for global limits on the debt of individual subnational jurisdictions on the basis of criteria that mimic market discipline (e.g., current and projected levels of debt service in relation to revenue using a comprehensive definition of debt subject to the ceiling). An alternative may be for the central government to set restrictions on transfers to local governments. However, administrative controls by central governments on subnational borrowing seem likely to conflict with the increasing trend worldwide toward devolution of spending and revenue raising responsibilities to subnational governments.

Finally, there is scope for increased cooperation at all levels of government in containing the growth of public debt and for greater involvement of subnational governments in formulating and implementing medium-term fiscal adjustment programs.[30] In this regard, it might be useful to bring the key players (e.g., the ministry of finance, the central bank, local governments) together in a multilateral forum to discuss budgetary policies and prospects of various government levels.

How the central government manages fiscal policy through revenue sharing, expenditure assignments, and transfers to local governments is a vast area in research. The experience of Estonia in the past few years illustrates some of the issues involved. Estonia began the transition to a market economy with a highly centralized system of public finances, local governments acting mainly as administrative units with no independent fiscal responsibility. Since then, it has made considerable progress in carrying out fiscal decentralization and, in particular, has promoted institutional settings and processes that

---

[30]Estonia adopted strenthened legislation to control local government borrowing in May 1997, and Latvia has already begun implementing similar reforms.

allow for the articulation of interests and policymaking based on consensus building. There has also been a move to match public services more closely with local demands. The design of transfers from the central to local governments, with its emphasis on equalization, attempts to place limits on the level of open-ended transfers that could create incentives to attract and self-generate local demand. Moreover, the transfer mechanism in Estonia has served to reduce the horizontal imbalances of the fiscal system: it lessens the fiscal disparities among local governments with different tax bases and closes the revenue gap of local governments (i.e., the imbalance between expenditure responsibilities and the funding available).

The system of intergovernmental relations in Estonia needs, however, to exploit more fully the benefits of fiscal decentralization. It must also ensure that local governments support the general effort to increase public saving and that budget constraints are enforced at each level of government. Given the passive role of local government over a 50-year period under Soviet times, this will require in part a concerted move to build up local capacity and a local civil service trained to design, monitor, and implement expenditure programs in its areas of responsibility. Against this backdrop, there are a number of steps that the authorities could take:

(1) Consolidation of local governments and increased cooperation among them in the delivery of public services would improve the efficiency of municipalities. The number of local governments in each of the Baltics is large (e.g., 254 in Estonia).

(2) For expenditure activities that are subject to overlapping or competing jurisdictions, the appropriate level of responsibility needs to be clarified.

(3) To increase the accountability of local governments and enhance their flexibility to meet the demand for services, a greater share of local expenditures should be financed with local taxes—as distinct from shared taxes, which represent a transfer from the central government (albeit out of an earmarked revenue source). Under the current system in Estonia, the proportion of local tax revenues (including transfers) under the control of municipalities is small, an average of 9 percent during 1993–96. One option for reform, already adopted in a number of countries, would be to give each local government the right to apply its own tax rate on the national income tax base. A local income tax surcharge would offer local governments a powerful revenue tool and increase the link, at least at the margin, between local public services and taxes

payable. This would not exclude the use of supplementary equalization transfers for poorer municipalities. Another option would be to increase municipal user fees.

(4) The new method for determining equalization transfers, while simpler and better at targeting local governments with per capita revenues lower than the national average, leaves the door open for considerable bargaining between the central government and individual municipalities—the Estonian authorities will have to ensure that such negotiations do not undermine the objective of reducing fiscal disparities across regions.

(5) The borrowing activities of local governments need to be better monitored and the legal restraints on debt obligations vigorously enforced. The central government has followed a rules-based approach to keeping municipal borrowing in check; one such rule restricts borrowing to investment projects. In practice, this approach proved to be inadequate owing mainly to the ambiguous wording of legislation, and to behavior aimed at circumventing the regulations (e.g., the reclassification of expenditures from current to capital, and the use of local government-owned enterprises to borrow for purposes that should be funded through the budget). The government has recently taken steps to address these problems, starting with a tightening of the law on municipal borrowing. Also, local governments must forward a copy of the decision to take a loan to the county governor within three days after it becomes effective, and send a copy of the loan contract to the Ministry of Finance within thirty days after the contract has been signed. In August 1996, the Government of Estonia issued a decree clarifying that the central government would not extend state guarantees—implicit or explicit—against municipal borrowing. And as of December 1997, the Bank of Estonia, as part of its prudential responsibilities over the banking system, requires that banking groups obtain in advance a letter of no objection from the Ministry of Finance (which will not represent either an explicit or implicit guarantee) for each additional financial claim acquired on local governments. By comparison, the other two Baltic countries have instituted strict administrative controls. In Latvia, local governments can borrow only from the treasury for investment projects deemed worthy, and in Lithuania, local governments can borrow to finance investment expenditures only after receiving central approval from a State Loan Commission.

References

Alesina, Alberto, and Roberto Perotti, 1996, "Budget Deficits and Budget Institutions," IMF Working Paper 96/52 (Washington: International Monetary Fund).

Banerjee, Biswajit, 1995, "The Transformation Path in the Czech Republic," *Road Maps of the Transition—The Baltics, the Czech Republic, Hungary and Russia,* IMF Occasional Paper No. 127 (Washington: International Monetary Fund).

Berengaut, Julian, and others, 1996, *Republic of Lithuania—Recent Economic Developments,* IMF Staff Country Report No. 96/72 (Washington: International Monetary Fund).

Chand, Sheetal K. and Henri Lorie, 1992, "Fiscal Policy," *Fiscal Policies in Economies in Transition,* ed. by Vito Tanzi (Washington: International Monetary Fund).

Chand, Sheetal K. and Albert Jaeger, 1996, *Aging Populations and Public Pension Schemes,* IMF Occasional Paper No. 147 (Washington: International Monetary Fund, December).

Cheasty, Adrienne, and Jeffrey M. Davis, 1996, "Fiscal Transition in Countries of the Former Soviet Union: An Interim Assessment," IMF Working Paper 96/61 (Washington: International Monetary Fund).

Chu, Ke-young and Sanjeev Gupta, 1996, "Social Protection in Transition Countries: Emerging Issues," IMF Paper on Policy Analysis and Assessment 96/5 (Washington: International Monetary Fund, May).

Fischer, Stanley, Ratna Sahay, and Carlos Végh, 1998, "How Far Is Eastern Europe From Brussels?" IMF Working Paper 98/53 (Washington: International Monetary Fund).

Garamfalvi, L., and W.A. Allan, 1996, "The Role of the Treasury in Public Expenditure Management in Selected OECD Countries," paper prepared for seminar on Transparency of Public Accounts, University of Bergamo, Italy, May.

Horton, Mark A., 1996, "Health and Education Expenditures in Russia, the Baltic States and the Other Countries of the Former Soviet Union," IMF Working Paper 96/126 (Washington: International Monetary Fund).

International Monetary Fund, 1996a, "Fiscal Challenges of Transition: Progress Made and Problems Remaining," Chapter V, *World Economic Outlook,* World Economic and Financial Surveys (Washington, May).

———, 1996b, "Long-Term Growth Potential in the Countries in Transition," Chapter V, *World Economic Outlook,* World Economic and Financial Surveys (Washington: International Monetary Fund, October).

James, Estelle, 1996, "New System for Old Age Security: Why, How and So What?" paper presented at EDI Conference on Pension Systems: From Crisis to Reform (Washington, November 21–22).

Lorie, Henri, and others, 1996, *Republic of Estonia—Selected Issues,* IMF Staff Country Report No. 96/96 (Washington: International Monetary Fund).

———, 1997, "Issues of Fiscal Sustainability in the Countries of the FSU: An Overview" (unpublished; Washington: International Monetary Fund).

Miles-Ferretti, Gian Maria, 1996, "Fiscal Rules and the Budget Process," IMF Working Paper 96/60 (Washington: International Monetary Fund).

Schwartz, Gerd, 1994, "Public Finances," in *Poland: The Path to a Market Economy,* IMF Occasional Paper No. 113 (Washington: International Monetary Fund).

Scott, Graham, 1996, *Government Reform in New Zealand,* IMF Occasional Paper No. 140 (Washington: International Monetary Fund).

Statistical Office of Estonia, 1996, *Statistical Yearbook of Estonia.*

Ter-Minassian, Teresa, 1996, "Borrowing by Subnational Governments: Issues and Selected International Experiences," IMF Paper on Policy Analysis and Assessment 96/4 (Washington: International Monetary Fund).

van der Mensbrugghe, Emmanuel, and others, 1996, *Republic of Latvia—Recent Economic Developments,* IMF Staff Country Report No. 96/43 (Washington: International Monetary Fund).

von Hagen, Jürgen, and Ian Harden, 1996, "Budget Processes and Commitment to Fiscal Discipline," IMF Working Paper 96/78 (Washington: International Monetary Fund).

World Bank, 1994, *Averting the Old Age Crisis: Policies to Protect the Old and Promote Growth* (Washington: World Bank and Oxford University Press).

———, 1995, *Estonia: Financing Local Governments,* Report No. 14925-EE (Washington: World Bank).

———, 1996, *World Development Report 1996, From Plan to Market* (Washington: Oxford University Press and the World Bank).

———, 1997, *Estonia: Public Expenditure Review Update,* Report No. 16420 EE (Washington: World Bank).

V   Financial System Issues in the Postcrisis Era

Effie Psalida

After regaining their independence in 1991 and introducing national currencies shortly thereafter, the Baltic countries undertook to stabilize their economies against a background of high inflation, large declines in output, and significant deterioration in their terms of trade.[1] The implementation of prudent financial policies has allowed the Baltic countries to achieve a steady decline in inflation since its peak in 1992 and to resume economic growth. Moreover, the first phase of transition has been completed in respect to structural reform, including price and trade liberalization and small-scale privatization.

As part of the transition to a market economy, the Baltic countries introduced major reforms in the financial sector, involving, in addition to the liberalization of the financial system, the buildup of institutions, expertise, markets, instruments, and changes in the legal and regulatory framework. During this period of financial liberalization and before a sound, market-based financial system was fully in place, all three experienced banking crises. These crises resulted from serious deficiencies in the internal management of banks, and the absence of an adequate regulatory and supervisory environment, both reflecting weaknesses in governance inherited from the planned economy of the Soviet Union.

Having weathered the banking crises, the Baltic countries have moved to face the challenges lying ahead in the area of financial sector reform. The authorities are taking the appropriate measures and giving the necessary signals for the resumption of financial market deepening. In each of the three countries, the banking sector has undergone systemic restructuring and in the process, ways have been found of dealing with bad loans and problem banks, and a healthy financial environment is being established to help prevent another crisis from taking place.

Background

Liberalization of the financial system inherited from the Soviet Union was accomplished early on in the reform period: subsidized and directed credits were almost completely phased out; controls on interest rates were removed; external current accounts became convertible; and almost all restrictions on capital movements were eliminated. Although financial deregulation has been largely completed, financial sector reforms are still continuing with efforts to develop a more competitive and sound banking system and an effective regulatory framework.

Early in the transition, in an effort aimed at developing a competitive and sound banking sector, the Baltic countries (1) established a two-tier banking system; (2) introduced central bank and commercial banking laws largely consistent with the requirements of a market economy; (3) incorporated and reorganized state-controlled banks; and (4) moved toward universal banking by mobilizing savings for all banks and developing skills for credit risk evaluation and portfolio selection. In the process of building up a market-based financial system, the Baltic countries have taken a number of important additional steps to build up considerable capacity for banking supervision; develop money, securities, and capital markets to facilitate the operations of the banking system and enhance monetary control; and set up efficient payments systems in which financial transactions can be effected quickly and safely.

During this period of financial liberalization and before an effective market-based financial system could be fully established, all Baltic countries underwent banking crises. Because of the low level of financial intermediation,[2] even the failure of large banks had limited systemic effects and a minor negative impact on output and incomes. The crises, however, slowed down the pace of financial reform by disrupting the process of financial development and reduced the banking system's role in credit intermediation.

The paper is a follow-up to "Financial Sector Reform and Banking Crises in the Baltic Countries" by Castello Branco, Kammer, and Psalida (1996).

[1]See Saavalainen (1995) for the Baltic countries' early record on stabilization.

[2]Wealth effects were small and investment demand was insensitive to the level of interest rates.

A positive effect of the banking crises was a consolidation of the banking system and the emergence of more cautious and prudent behavior among surviving banks, as the financial system retrenched before resuming financial deepening. As of the end of 1997, there were 11 banks in Estonia, 31 in Latvia, and 11 in Lithuania, down from a peak of 43, 63, and 28, respectively (Figure 5.1). These numbers do not include a foreign bank branch each in Estonia and Latvia and several representative offices in Estonia and Lithuania. In addition, all three Baltic countries have operating and growing stock exchanges, as well as a growing number of licensed financial intermediaries and brokers.

The development of money markets and monetary control procedures followed different paths in the Baltic countries. In respect to the interbank market, Estonia developed an important vehicle for managing day-to-day liquidity; already in 1994 the daily volume of transactions exceeded 1 percent of reserve money and interest rate trends followed closely the interbank money market rate. By contrast, in Latvia and in Lithuania transactions on the interbank market peaked at ½ of 1 percent of reserve money in December 1994 and in the summer of 1995, respectively, before activity declined as banking problems surfaced; activity picked up again in 1996.

Indirect instruments of monetary policy have also been introduced as part of the reforms. Money markets are still underdeveloped and the shift toward market based monetary policy is by no means complete. With the adoption of currency board arrangements (CBAs), in Estonia in 1992 and Lithuania in 1994 discretionary monetary policy was effectively ruled out.[3] Given the central banks' limited experience in formulating and implementing monetary policy, a currency board rule allowed the central banks to devote more of their resources to developing banking regulations and improving monitoring of the banking system.

Both Latvia and Lithuania have successfully established a primary market in treasury bills through an auction procedure.[4] Amounts outstanding have increased steadily since their introduction in December

---

[3]For the operation of the currency board arrangement in Estonia, see Bennett (1992) and (1994). Camard (1996) describes the process leading up to the establishment of the currency board arrangement in Lithuania and the country's early experience with it. See also Berengaut and others (1996) for a discussion of Lithuania's experiences under the currency board arrangement.

[4]Treasury bills have not been issued in Estonia as there has been limited need for domestic financing of the budget.

Figure 5.1. Number of Banks[1]

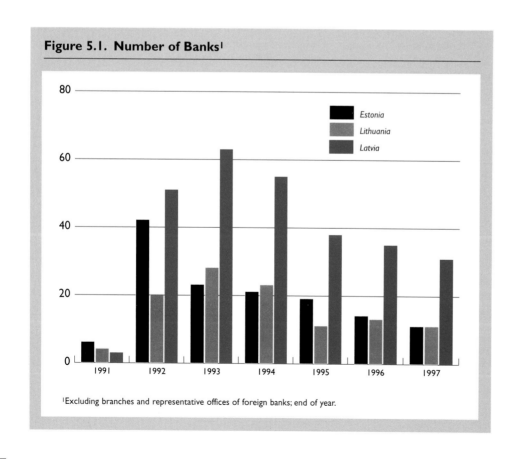

[1]Excluding branches and representative offices of foreign banks; end of year.

1993 and July 1994, respectively, except in the context of the banking crises, when there was a substantial weakening in demand for bills reflecting banks' liquidity problems. A few months after the crises, however, demand rebounded in each of the two countries as banks opted for holding safe and liquid treasury bills rather than offering credit to the private sector.

Financial Deepening and Financial Intermediation

If the Baltic countries were to seek to broaden their options for conducting monetary policy, they would need to rely further on indirect instruments of monetary control. At the same time, the financial systems would need to play the role of generating saving and directing it to productive use. To meet this dual challenge and facilitate the economy's move toward greater financial intermediation, the financial system would have to become deeper and broader, and at the same time remain stable.

Financial sector developments during the period leading up to the banking crises were characterized by an initial increase in the number of banks, in the ratio of money to GDP, and in the holdings of financial assets by the private sector.[5] At the same time, there was a decline in the ratio of currency to deposits and in the banks' reserve-to-deposit ratio, leading to an increase in the money multiplier. One of the consequences of the banking crises was the disruption of these trends and thus the slowdown or reversal of the modest amount of financial deepening that had begun during the early reform period (Figures 5.2–5.4). The Baltic countries now face the challenge of resuming the process of increasing financial deepening and intermediation.

The remonetization of the Baltic economies must come about with a shift in the demand for money, which will require improved public confidence in the financial system. Despite early and fast financial deregulation, the role taken on by the banking sector in financial intermediation has been modest. Banks are far from playing a comparable role to those in other transition economies of central and eastern Europe (Table 5.1). The required confidence has been slow in coming: in Latvia and in Lithuania, where the banking systems are still dealing with the effects of the banking crises,[6] the currency-to-deposit ratio,

which followed an upward trend after the crises, remains high as economic agents continue to rely heavily on the use of cash for transactions and deposits have declined as a ratio to GDP. In Latvia, which experienced its banking crisis and took a number of policy measures before Lithuania, a moderate resumption of financial deepening began in the third quarter of 1996. Even more so in Estonia, there has been steady growth of credit and deposits as percent of GDP, which began in the aftermath of the banking crisis of 1992 (Figure 5.5).

The return of confidence will allow interest rates to begin to play a more important role as price signals in the market and increase incentives for the public to participate in financial intermediation. The process is further advanced in Estonia than in Latvia, and somewhat less in Lithuania. In all three countries, nominal interest rates originally responded sluggishly to the decline in inflation, which is not uncommon when interest rates are liberalized rapidly and early in the reform process, before significant progress has been made in enterprise and financial sector reform and while effective banking supervision is not yet in place. The persistence of large interest rate margins between foreign currency and domestic currency loans and deposits, and between lending and deposit rates reflected (1) the uncertainty surrounding the nature of capital inflows; (2) high default premiums; (3) banks' attempts to recapitalize; and (4) large stocks of nonperforming assets in banks' portfolios. These margins—relevant particularly in Latvia and Lithuania—contributed to financial instability and had a negative impact on investment and growth.

Despite their originally sluggish response, bank interest rates are increasingly reflecting economic conditions. In 1996, Latvia experienced a declining trend in market rates following lower inflation, positive fiscal developments, and stabilization in the financial market, including the publication of improved annual audit reports for commercial banks. Interest rates in Lithuania, after an initial doubling immediately following the banking crisis in early 1996, were on a sharp and continuous declining trend through the end of the year and during much of 1997. Spreads between lending and deposit rates have also been declining in the Baltic countries (Figure 5.6).

Development of the Money, Securities, and Capital Markets

Although the financial sector in the Baltic countries has so far been dominated by commercial banking, some inroads are being made toward the establishment of more mature money, securities, and

---

[5]Castello Branco, Kammer, and Psalida (1996) contains a detailed discussion of financial sector reform in the Baltic countries after they regained independence.

[6]The banking crises took place in Latvia in the spring of 1995, in Lithuania in late 1995/early 1996; Estonia experienced a major crisis in 1992 and a lesser one in 1994.

Figure 5.2. Indicators of Financial Intermediation I

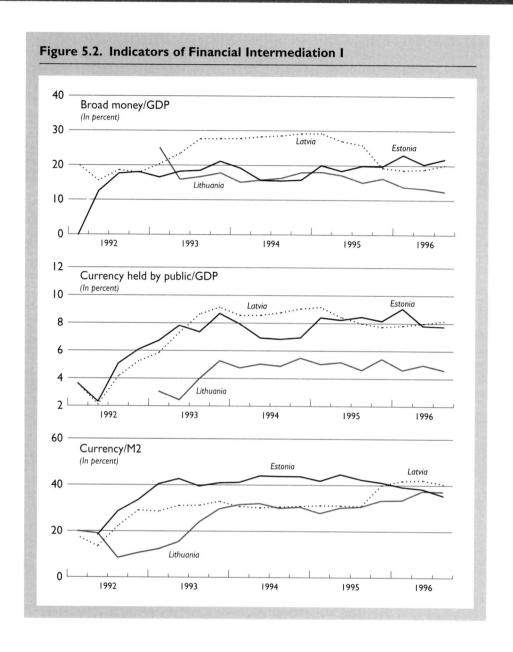

capital markets. The desire to develop these markets further and to increase monetary policy options must, however, proceed with caution and after a period of adequate preparation intended to protect economic agents from destabilizing surprises. Progress must be made in the continuing improvement of the financial condition of the banking sector and the restoration of the public's confidence in it. In turn, the establishment of confidence will help develop the financial markets.

The central bank of Latvia offers three types of loans to banks, namely, daily repurchase auctions, an automatic overnight Lombard window, and longer-term Lombard credits, and two mechanisms for with-

drawing liquidity, nonnegotiable deposits and reverse repurchase agreements. Despite the availability of instruments, however, the level of activity has been low as most banks have been pursuing a cautious approach following the banking crisis and, after the immediate period following the crisis, there has not been a need for liquidity injection because of balance of payments surpluses. In Estonia and in Lithuania, where the CBA limits the central bank's monetary operations, monetary instruments until recently have been nonexistent or dormant. Lithuania has introduced some monetary operations (treasury bill repurchase operations, deposits auctions) to build up its institutional capabilities prior to its eventual intro-

Figure 5.3. Indicators of Financial Intermediation II

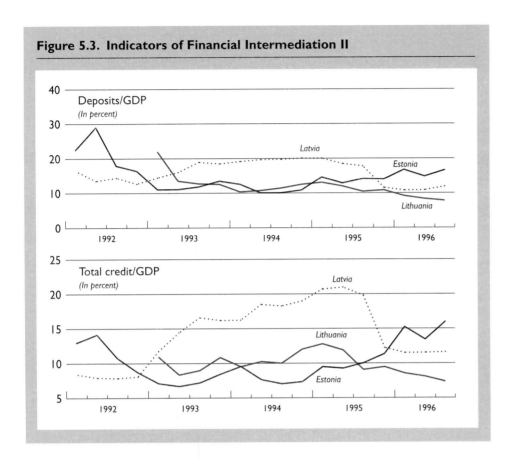

duction of a monetary policy regime that would allow for a greater degree of policy discretion.

Within the constraints of the CBA, the interbank market in Estonia has become an important vehicle for managing banks' day-to-day liquidity. As banks gained experience in evaluating counterparty risk and became familiar with each other, they depended less on the use of collateral (certificates of deposit issued by the central bank); consequently, most interbank activity is now uncollateralized. In Latvia and in Lithuania, the interbank market is now showing some signs of growth, especially in Latvia; before it had always been thin and virtually collapsed around the time of the banking crises. With the tightened enforcement of prudential requirements and the increased familiarity with other banks' financial position, banks are more willing to lend to each other, although the market is still thin and volatile.

In the aftermath of the banking crises in Latvia and Lithuania and following the immediate postcrisis period of low bank liquidity, activity in the primary market for treasury bills has surged, a direct result of the cautious approach followed by banks reluctant to lend in a fragile and potentially volatile environment. As a result, primary auctions have become more

competitive, making interest rates more stable, especially in Latvia (Figure 5.7).[7] At the same time, the primary market for government securities is becoming deeper and broader with the introduction of longer maturity paper and the availability of one-month, three-month, six-month, and one-year maturities on a regular basis in Latvia and also increasingly in Lithuania. The availability of longer maturities is also likely to boost activity further in the secondary market, which has been increasing in both countries. In Lithuania, where securities traded before maturity are subject to tax but others are not, a change in the tax treatment would also contribute to the development of a smoother and more active market.

As the money and securities markets develop, the authorities should be mindful of the reduced effectiveness of such instruments when weaknesses in banks' loan portfolios or management lead to interbank market segmentation and make banks unresponsive to price signals.[8] Market segmentation oc-

[7]See van der Mensbrugghe (1996) for more detail.

[8]See Lindgren, Garcia, and Saal (1996) for a detailed discussion of the effects of bank soundness on the conduct of monetary policy.

Figure 5.4. Money Multiplier

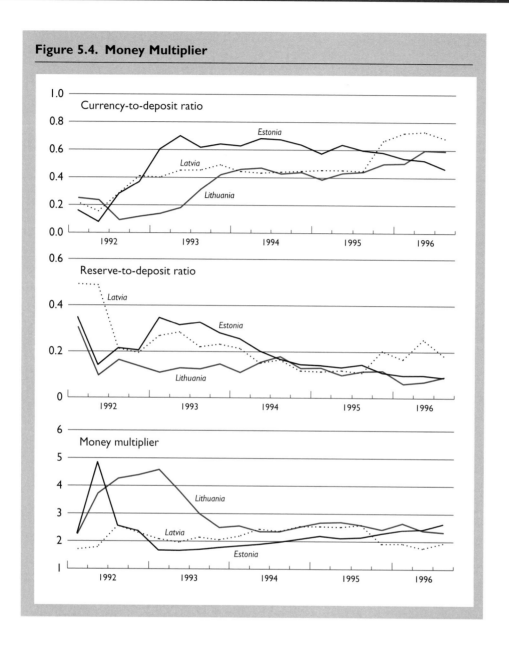

curs when sound banks receive a disproportionate amount of deposits, which, in their attempt to retain safe and liquid assets and to cut their exposure to risk, they invest in treasury bills whose yields tend to decline. At the same time, unsound banks, which may not have access to interbank borrowing, may face shortfalls in their required reserves and overdrafts in their clearing accounts and be forced to resort to distress borrowing. Such a situation can complicate the development of market-based instruments and distort interest rates.

For the effective implementation of monetary instruments, preparation and testing will be required to ensure that the technical arrangements are fully adequate and sufficient institutional capacity is in place

at the central banks. A full framework must exist at the central banks for the analysis and forecasting of conditions affecting the central bank balance sheets and the markets in which they will operate. More important, the authorities must feel that monetary policy should be conducted in a context of central bank independence and with a clear mandate to enforce price stability.

The domestic capital market in the Baltic countries started from a low base and has been slow to develop due to credit constraints and insufficient depth in the financial system. During the initial years of reform and before sufficient macroeconomic stability, the uncertainty and volatility of the markets and the level of real interest rates were excessively high and

Table 5.1. Indicators of Financial Intermediation (End-1997)

	Broad Money/GDP	Bank Claims on Private Sector/GDP	Deposits/GDP
Estonia	31	35	24
Latvia	26	11	16
Lithuania	20	12	13
Other central and eastern Europe (end-1995)[1]	55	35	45
Poland	40	24	33
OECD (end-1995)[1]	75	90	70

[1]Pazarbaşıoğlu and van der Vossen (1997).

had a negative impact on investment. Later on, although real interest rates declined and, in some cases, became negative, credit availability remained low, as most enterprises either lacked the collateral or a long enough credit history. The problem was compounded by the lack of an established legal and institutional basis on which the use of collateral could develop.[9] In this context, it is important to recognize the links between structural reform in the enterprise sector and in the financial sector, and that unless reform progresses in all sectors of the econ-

[9]Land registers, for example, did not exist.

Figure 5.5 Credit and Deposit Growth
(In Percent)

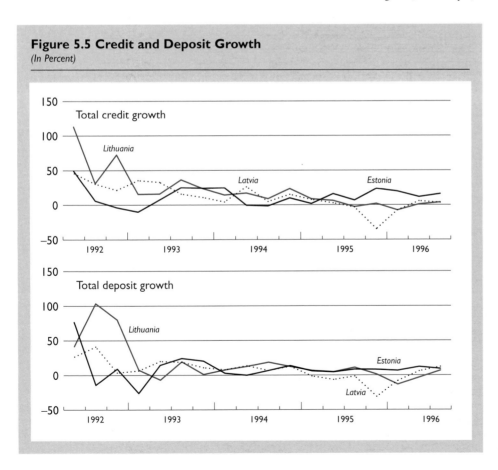

Figure 5.6. Interest Rates

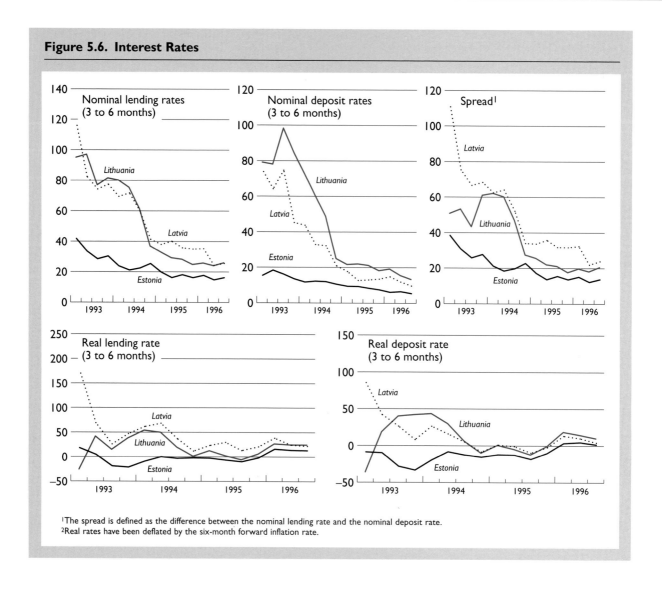

¹The spread is defined as the difference between the nominal lending rate and the nominal deposit rate.
²Real rates have been deflated by the six-month forward inflation rate.

omy, structural bottlenecks can have substantial spill-over effects.

The availability of foreign capital in the Baltic countries has often filled the gap where domestic capital has been in short supply, especially in Estonia and Latvia where foreign direct investment, at least until 1996, has been higher than in Lithuania.

Restructuring the Banking System

After having experienced "structural" banking crises, the Baltic countries have had to restructure their banking sectors so as to render them viable and allow them a more active role in financial intermediation. As a first step, this has implied finding ways to deal with the stock of bad loans and problem banks. As a second step, it has meant establishing a healthy

financial environment that would help prevent another crisis from happening. In addressing both issues, the Baltic authorities will face a number of constraints, and the path they follow could have different implications for the near and longer term.

Addressing the Stock Dimension of the Problem

In deciding how to deal with the stock of bad loans and the questionable viability of problem banks, the authorities in the Baltic countries have had to weigh whether or not to bail out banks or creditors, or both. Aspects to consider in these decisions concern questions of contagion, moral hazard, helping build public confidence, fiscal costs, and consequences of government ownership of banks and eventual privatization. A related issue has been examining the

Figure 5.7. Treasury Bill Rates
(In percent)

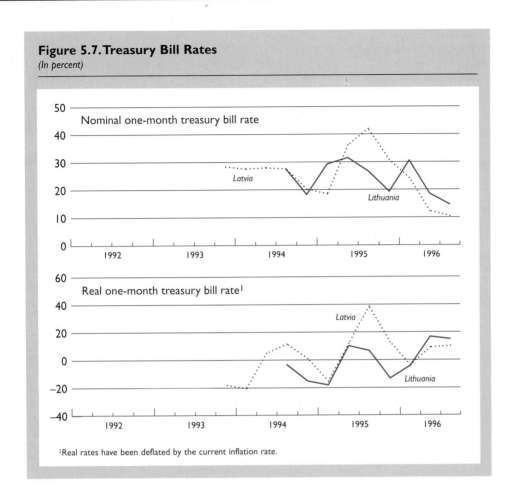

¹Real rates have been deflated by the current inflation rate.

advantages of a centralized loan-recovery agency, as opposed to leaving it up to the individual banks to recover bad loans.

An advantage of direct financial assistance by the government in addressing the stock of nonperforming loans and the solvency and liquidity problems of banks is that budgetary costs are transparent. Such assistance has taken many forms, including acquisition of bad loans (Estonia and Lithuania), recapitalization schemes (all three countries), assisted mergers (Estonia), and liquidity support (all three countries).

The experience of the Baltic countries has shown that minimizing bailouts contributes to boosting the public's confidence in the banking system; it builds trust that the central bank will back only viable banks and that the authorities in general will not support problematic entities that will drain the system indefinitely. In this context, the no-bailout approach also reduces moral hazard by helping to contain the flow problem. In Estonia, which was the first to experience banking problems, the authorities dealt quite differently with the 1992 and the 1994 episodes. In the earlier crisis, after initial liquidity

support when the crisis was thought to be temporary, the central bank moved quickly to close the problem banks and to deal with them in a decisive manner—in one case, without bailing out creditors.[10] In contrast, the Social Bank crisis of 1994 dragged on for a year, drained large resources from the central bank (equivalent to 6 percent of base money), and, with the exception of shareholders, created no losses to creditors who were bailed out at government expense. In Latvia, after Bank Baltija had become insolvent in early 1995 and had received one emergency liquidity loan from the central bank, its operations were suspended and it entered bankruptcy and liquidation procedures. Creditors received no bail-out of any kind despite the size of the bank (it accounted for 30 percent of deposits of the banking system) and the extent of its complex connections.

In Lithuania, on the other hand, the authorities did not show the same resolve in dealing with the larger banks that they had shown with problematic small banks. Moreover, the implementation of measures to strengthen the banking system, following the sus-

───────

[10]For more detail see Knöbl (1993).

pension of operations of Innovation Bank and Litim-peks Bank in December 1995, was delayed repeatedly. The ensuing political turmoil, a number of contradictory laws passed by parliament, and the initial inaction of the authorities concerning the affected banks further undermined the public's confidence in the financial system. For instance, it took more than a year after its operations were suspended and after it came under its full control for the government to decide to liquidate Innovation Bank.

In addition to questions of moral hazard and the building of public confidence, bailing out problem banks can imply large and open-ended expenditures for the government budget and the central bank, as was the case with Estonia in 1994. An alternative approach followed in Latvia, Lithuania, and Estonia (in 1992) was for the government to issue long-term bonds to replace nonperforming loans in state-controlled banks and to recapitalize these banks.[11] In Lithuania, current costs of this scheme amount to interest payments on the long-term restructuring bonds, whose rates are based on the average interest rate in banks' term deposits plus 1 percentage point; at the end of the ten-year maturity the principal is expected to be rolled over.

Following the banking crises, the government or the central bank assumed control of banks that had required direct financial government support. This was not so in Latvia, where the banking sector had become predominantly private early on in the transition and where the government by and large refrained from supporting the banking sector financially during the crisis. In Estonia and Lithuania, however, state involvement in bank ownership brought on the government the responsibility for eventual privatization, which presented a number of challenges, including asset valuation, especially for banks that have questionable loan portfolios, and finding appropriate private owners given banks' special systemic vulnerability and issues of contagion effects.

Establishing a proper market value for a bank can be especially difficult with a lack of proper accounting on the part of debtor enterprises, a problem that has been present in all three countries; as a result, legitimate potential buyers can be in short supply. In Estonia, privatization of the three state-controlled banks following the crises took the form of either an increase in total equity by sale to private investors or the partial sale of existing equity held by the state; the process included aggressive restructuring and mergers. The result was the gradual privatization of

the state banks, with the central bank guiding the process to ensure that privatization proceeded smoothly and systemic risks were minimized.[12] A year after the outbreak of the banking crisis in Lithuania, the government increased its ownership share in the three state-controlled banks and now owns what used to be the largest private bank before the crisis. The authorities now face the multiple challenge of restructuring, rendering viable, and privatizing these banks as part of their effort to modernize the financial system with a view to eventual accession to the EU.

The consolidation of the banking sector that followed the closure of banks during the banking crises in the Baltic countries has been desirable, given the large number of nonviable banks that had sprung up early in the reform because of liberal licensing policies and low minimum capital requirements. Care should be taken, however, that the number of banks does not go below the minimum number required to foster a competitive banking sector.

Addressing the Flow Dimension of the Problem

Experience in the Baltic countries confirms that recapitalization of banks cannot be successful without simultaneously restructuring the banking sector, since the proper incentives are not created for avoiding the accumulation of new bad loans. In addition to handling the stock of bad debt, in facing the challenge of building a stable and well-functioning banking system, the Baltic authorities will have to (1) adhere to a consistently strict enforcement of prudential regulations while improving other aspects of banking supervision; (2) move ahead with restructuring the enterprise sector so as to open up sound investment opportunities for banks; and (3) develop an appropriate legal framework for the overall economic environment. This must be done in the context of continued fiscal restraint so that resources can be freed to the private sector.

Although banking supervision alone may not have been able to prevent the banking crises in the Baltic countries, strict enforcement of prudential regulations and closer monitoring would have reduced their magnitude. The formal establishment of prudential regulations (Table 5.2) did not guarantee their effectiveness. In particular, although insider and connected lending was formally limited in 1994 in all three countries, these limits have been either disregarded or actively circumvented as became evident from the major bank collapses. Given the close ties between companies and banks, a legacy inher-

---

[11]In Estonia and Latvia, the value of the long-term bonds amounted to about 2½ percent of GDP; in Lithuania, where the value of bad loans transferred was after full provision for losses, the value did not exceed ½ of 1 percent of GDP.

[12]See Lorie (1996) for more details.

Table 5.2 Prudential Regulations and Deposit Protection

	Estonia	Latvia	Lithuania
Prudential regulations			
Minimum capital requirement (January 1, 1998)	EEK 75 million (ECU 5 million)	LVL 1 million[1] (ECU 1.4 million)	LTL 24.2 million (ECU 5 million)
Maximum connected lending	20 percent of bank's capital	15 percent of bank's capital	10 percent of bank's capital
Maximum lending to a single borrower	25 percent of bank's capital	25 percent of bank's capital	25 percent of bank's capital
Maximum foreign exchange exposure	From 1996, there are no special limits[2]		
Overall open position		20 percent of bank's capital	30 percent of bank's capital
Any one currency		10 percent of bank's capital	20 percent of bank's capital
Deposit protection (January 1, 1998)	Law submitted to parliament	Proposal with parliament	Up to LTL 25,000 (US$6,250) per deposit account

[1]LVL 2 million on April 1, 1998 for new banks, January 1, 1999 for all banks.
[2]Foreign exchange risk is covered by the regulation on capital adequacy, although there are limits on "Zone B" currencies (e.g., ruble, lats).

ited from the Soviet system and still in effect to some degree, it is particularly important that insider and connected lending limits be strictly enforced in the future.

The smooth function of a market-based financial system and the effectiveness of indirect instruments depend decisively on a consistent and stable valuation of financial assets. In addition to dealing with the stock of nonperforming loans, this can be achieved by adhering to international accounting standards and prudential norms. After the adoption of international accounting standards and the calculation of the capital base, according to the definition of the Bank for International Settlements (BIS), by Lithuania at the end of 1996, all three Baltic countries are now on board. The process of developing a system of adequate financial risk management is far from being complete, however.[13] The Baltic authorities, as part of their consolidation of financial market development, must strengthen the supervision of securities and capital market activities of banks and foster the establishment of well-capitalized and well-supervised financial dealerships.[14]

The degree of maximum foreign exchange exposure can have strong performance implications for banks that have become accustomed to strictly fixed exchange rates under either a CBA (Estonia and Lithuania) or a rate tied to the SDR (Latvia) if the Baltic authorities decide to move to more flexible exchange rate arrangements in the future. In this context, the manner and timing of a change in the exchange rate regime, as well as the degree of banks' foreign currency exposure, can be a substantial source of shock to individual banks.

In addition to the enforcement of prudential regulations (external governance), the Baltic banks will be required to develop strict internal control procedures and practices to govern operations and to ensure that they function in a safe and sound manner (internal governance). This will require that Baltic banks diversify their portfolios, develop further their credit evaluation skills, improve their accounting systems, and eliminate fraud. The quality of existing internal governance is not homogeneous across banks or countries. Certain banks (particularly state-controlled) need to undergo major adjustment in respect to political interference in lending, poor management, and insider lending, while other banks are functioning under strict market conditions.

An area in which there is pressing need for transparency and consistency for a smooth functioning of the banking system is the legal framework, particu-

[13]The role of the European Bank for Reconstruction and Development (EBRD) and the formation of "twinning arrangements" between individual Baltic commercial banks and established commercial banks abroad have advanced this process.

[14]See Sundararajan (1996) for a discussion of prudential supervision and financial restructuring during the transition.

larly as it applies to the use of collateral and bankruptcy laws. Although bankruptcy laws are effective on paper, they are still being tested in practice.[15] Transparent and stable laws and regulations on banking and investment will also facilitate the entry of foreign financial institutions into the Baltic countries, a process that can provide quickly the much needed capital and know-how to the financial sector.

Looking Ahead

After having confronted the banking crises, the Baltic countries took a number of important measures to safeguard the health of the financial system and to help prevent another crisis from happening. Restructuring activity, prudential norms, and supervisory procedures have been refined and modified according to the level of market development and of the governance of financial institutions. As more experience is gained, the Baltic countries are making inroads in financial intermediation and consolidating the development of their financial markets.

The three Baltic countries, however, are not at the same stage in the development of their financial systems. Estonia, being the first to have experienced a banking crisis, has also made the most progress in consolidating its banking system and in returning gradually to a trend of increasing financial deepening; on the other hand, the existence of the currency board arrangement has restricted the development of money markets, as has also happened in Lithuania. Latvia, which may avail itself to a number of monetary instruments, has made only modest use of them so far. At the same time, as the public regains confidence in the banking system, financial intermediation in Latvia is increasing. Lithuania is still implementing its bank-restructuring program following the banking crisis. Despite the banking crises and the different degrees of government and central bank involvement in them, the three Baltic countries have maintained a tight fiscal policy even if one includes long-term government debt issued to restructure the banking system.

The experience of Estonia has shown that resuming trends of financial deepening and increasing financial intermediation occurs slowly. The authorities can facilitate the process by adopting appropriate measures, but regaining confidence cannot be rushed. The parallel strengthening of internal and external governance of banks is likewise slow. In the meantime, the financial sectors in the Baltic countries remain fragile. A pertinent, though not necessarily speculative, question thus becomes: What could be the source of a future crisis? Even if there are no evident answers, one can identify several considerations that are relevant to the Baltic financial systems:

- residual fragility in the banking system;
- the possibility of rapid growth of credit against the backdrop of slow growth in the enterprise sector;
- risks of reappearance of macroeconomic imbalances and serious external shocks; and
- the possibility of asset bubbles (e.g., rising prices of real estate or stock shares used for collateral when borrowing to purchase additional real estate or stock shares).

As banks vie for position in claiming the profitable opportunities in the economy, competitive pressures may increase to the point that decisions are made based on expectations of rapid economic growth and underestimation of the risks involved in asset-based lending. Recent rapid rises in the Baltic stock markets may not necessarily be based on sustainable economic fundamentals. As the experience of the Nordic countries in the late 1980s and early 1990s has shown, a number of distortions and structural rigidities following rapid liberalization may magnify the impact of a negative shock to the system and put the stability of the whole financial system at risk.[16] The Baltic countries may be vulnerable to such banking crises of a more traditional nature.

Before the Baltic financial systems reach a critical point of stability and maturity, they remain vulnerable to macroeconomic imbalances or exogenous shocks. Such a shock may materialize for instance in the form of a crisis in a large neighboring country, which may then motivate the massive exodus from the Baltic countries of foreign capital, in the form of foreign direct investment, foreign share participation in financial and other institutions, or foreign participation in Baltic government securities.

References

Bennett, Adam, 1992, "The Operation of the Estonian Currency Board," IMF Paper on Policy Analysis and Assessment 92/3 (Washington: International Monetary Fund).

———, 1994, "Currency Boards: Issues and Experiences," IMF Paper on Policy Analysis and Assessment 94/18 (Washington: International Monetary Fund).

---

[15]A general bankruptcy law was introduced in Estonia in 1992, while bankruptcy procedures for banks became effective in Lithuania in 1994 and in Latvia in 1996.

---

[16]See Drees and Pazarbaşıoğlu (1995).

Berengaut, Julian, and others, 1996, *Republic of Lithuania—Recent Economic Developments,* IMF Staff Country Report No. 96/72 (Washington: International Monetary Fund).

Camard, Wayne, 1996, "Discretion with Rules? Lessons from the Currency Board Arrangement in Lithuania," IMF Paper on Policy Analysis and Assessment 96/1 (Washington: International Monetary Fund).

Castello Branco, Marta de, Alfred Kammer, and L. Effie Psalida, 1996, "Financial Sector Reform and Banking Crises in the Baltic Countries," IMF Working Paper 96/134 (Washington: International Monetary Fund).

Drees, Burkhard, and Ceyla Pazarbaşıoğlu, 1995, "The Nordic Banking Crises: Pitfalls in Financial Liberalization?" IMF Working Paper 95/61 (Washington: International Monetary Fund).

Knöbl, Adalbert, and others, 1993, *Republic of Estonia,* IMF Economic Review No. 4 (Washington: International Monetary Fund).

Lindgren, Carl-Johan, Gillian Garcia, and Matthew I. Saal, 1996, *Bank Soundness and Macroeconomic Policy* (Washington: International Monetary Fund).

Lorie, Henri, and others, 1996, *Republic of Estonia—Selected Issues,* IMF Staff Country Report No. 96/96 (Washington: International Monetary Fund).

Pazarbaşıoğlu, Ceyla and J.W. van der Vossen, 1997, "Design of Bank Restructuring Strategies in the Baltic States and the CIS: Main Issues and Challenges," *Central Bank Reform in the Transition Economies,* ed. by Sundararajan, V., Arne Petersen, and Gabriel Sensenbrenner (Washington: International Monetary Fund).

Saavalainen, Tapio O., 1995, "Stabilization in the Baltic Countries: Early Experience," *Road Maps of the Transition,* IMF Occasional Paper No. 127 (Washington: International Monetary Fund).

Sundararajan, V., 1996, "The Role of Prudential Supervision and Financial Restructuring of Banks During Transition to Indirect Instruments of Monetary Control," IMF Working Paper 96/128 (Washington: International Monetary Fund).

van der Mensbrugghe, Emmanuel, and others, 1996, *Republic of Latvia—Recent Economic Developments,* IMF Staff Country Report No. 96/287 (Washington: International Monetary Fund).

VI Private Sector Development

Richard Stern

To address the issue of private sector development in the Baltic countries, many economists have focused on privatization, assuming that it is a proxy for private sector development. But as the experience of countries such as Poland has revealed, privatization, though important, is only part of the story. Here, a more comprehensive approach is taken; the development of the private sector is considered the nexus of a policy agenda that establishes a solid legal and institutional framework and promotes both privatization and growth of capital markets. It is argued that obstacles to private sector growth stem from inadequate legal and institutional frameworks and from barriers to the development of capital markets. Though the analysis focuses on the Baltic countries, the main conclusions might be applicable to other countries in transition as well.

Methodological Issues: Definitions and Measurement Biases

Why should attention be paid to the development of the private sector? It is clear that the development of the private sector in itself is not a sufficient condition for high levels of economic growth. Rather, private sector development is interpreted as an "index" of the progress made in a transition economy from central planning to market-driven allocation of resources. It is argued below that the development of the private sector depends on the development of strong legal and institutional frameworks as well as the continued widening and deepening of capital markets. Both conditions are signs of strong progress during the transition. Thus, private sector development can be interpreted as a proxy indicator of the extent of progress during the transition process.

A fundamental issue facing the study of private sector development is determining what is private and what is not. This issue has both micro- (firm level) and macroeconomic (aggregate) dimensions. At the micro level, for example, is a firm that has gone through privatization and has had only 30 percent of its assets transferred to private hands to be considered private or still in the state sector? From a political standpoint, the firm may be called private by the government (perhaps to fulfill quantitative privatization targets), although effective control is still in the hands of the state. At the macro level is the additional problem that countries might define the private sector differently. Most countries consider the private sector to be the "nonstate" sector. But state-owned enterprises might be considered nonstate, thus overestimating the extent of private sector development. Therefore, even with strict guidelines defining what is private and what is not, the measurements, especially at the macro level, are imprecise at best. For this paper, the private sector is defined as the "nonstate sector"; thus firms whose assets have been even partially divested by the state are considered private.

The two most common measures of private sector development are total output by the private sector as a proportion of GDP and employment in the private sector as a percentage of total employment. Both of these measures are imperfect. As regards the output-GDP measure, at the macro level it is commonly accepted that official statistics in transition economies do not fully capture private sector activity. Some of the activity is hidden to avoid taxation. Thus it is reasonable to assume that the actual level of output generated by the private sector is actually higher than reported. At the same time, private sector development measured by output contribution magnifies the importance of private sector development in general. In most transition economies, the source of private sector development is primarily the entry of new, small businesses—predominantly in the service sector (such as catering and tourism) as well as small-scale retail trade. In the data, it might appear that private sector development is large because the growth of small businesses measured as a percentage of GDP is magnified by the simultaneous sectoral output declines in manufactured goods, industrial production in general, and agriculture both in terms of volume and employment. Thus, the data are biased upward owing to the rise of small firms, and not necessarily owing to private sector control of traditionally large sectors (large as a percentage of GDP), such as heavy industry and manufacturing.

The employment measure also has its biases. First, this measurement might understate the true private sector contribution to the economy because in most cases, a private firm would use less labor than its state-owned counterpart, such that the number of workers may be low but total output may be high. Thus the greater efficiency of the private sector (in theory) suggests a lower number of workers (i.e., productivity of labor is higher in the private sector) than in a comparable state sector firm. The other problem is again under-reporting. To avoid social contributions (on the firm side) and income tax (on the worker side), a worker's labor may go unreported and therefore the total number of workers employed in the private sector might be understated.

Progress in Private Sector Development

According to EBRD estimates, private sector activity has grown rapidly, as measured in percent of total GDP and in percent of total employment. These figures compare favorably with the Czech Republic (75 percent of total GDP in 1997), Poland (65 percent of total GDP in 1997), and Russia (70 percent of GDP in 1997) (see Table 6.1). As noted above, the figures might be misleading, given the differences in definition of what constitutes private versus state sectors, as well as the caveats stated above regarding measurement. In Latvia, for example, the bulk of private sector activity is in agriculture, construction, and services (especially retail trade and financial in-

termediation), whereas in industry, most of the production is still in state hands.

Necessary Conditions for Private Sector Development

Three conditions are necessary but not sufficient individually to generate private sector development:[1]
- institutional foundations to create the environment conducive to private sector development;
- privatization; and
- availability of capital, or development of domestic capital markets.

It is argued here that the absence of these conditions imposes barriers to private sector development.

To date, most countries in transition have not fully met these conditions for private sector development; as a result, the ability of the private sector to grow has been constrained. In many cases, economic policy has explicitly impeded or prevented the development of at least one of these conditions. Where the impediments have been removed eventually, valuable time has been lost and private sector development was substantially inhibited.

At the same time, cross country analysis indicates that there is no clear optimal order of sequencing of these conditions. Many countries (such as the Czech Republic and Russia) chose to begin economic reform with privatization as the centerpiece; whereas

---

[1]Assuming that macroeconomic foundations (price liberalization and stabilization that followed the freeing of prices) are already largely in place.

Table 6.1. Measurement of Private Sector Development
(Percent)

Country	1991	1992	1993	1994	1995	1996	1997
Estonia							
Percent of GDP	18[1]	45	51	58	65	70	70
Percent of total employment	11	15	...	...	...	...	...
Latvia							
Percent of GDP	...	...	...	50	58	60	65
Percent of total employment	12	31	47	53	58	...	...
Lithuania							
Percent of GDP	16	37	57	62	65	65	70
Percent of total employment	...	...	...	...	...	...	...

Source: EBRD (1995, 1996).
[1]This figure is defined as pure private sector, whereas all other figures are defined as nonstate sector unless otherwise noted.

others (Poland, Estonia, and Latvia) chose to set up the institutional foundations first before privatization. All have found that the shortage of capital (domestic and foreign), due either to microeconomic credit constraints or to insufficient financial market depth and breadth, has been a binding constraint on private sector development.

Institutional Environment Conducive to Private Sector Development

As the backbone of private sector development, a consistent and comprehensive legal framework allows entrepreneurs to know the "rules of the game" to make rational investment and production choices. Not only does this necessary condition require the adoption of laws and commercial codes, but it also requires that the legal framework be implemented in practice. Many countries, including Latvia and Lithuania, have adopted the necessary legal infrastructure but have been slow in implementation, resulting in commensurately slow private sector development and low levels of foreign direct investment.

At a minimum, a legal framework capable of fostering the development of the private sector requires:
- a set of laws governing the incorporation of firms;
- a transparent commercial code;
- a competition policy and institutions dealing with competition issues;
- a consistent set of laws governing all aspects of privatization;
- a set of laws governing land reform and ownership;
- clear bankruptcy legislation;
- laws defining the legal rights of foreign participants in the domestic market; and
- laws governing foreign investment.

In most transition countries, including the Baltics, the problem is less the adoption of the laws than their implementation. Bankruptcy laws in particular have been slow to be adopted and rarely enforced.

Privatization

Countries such as Poland have shown that privatization in itself is not a sufficient condition for private sector development.[2] At the same time, privatization is a signal that the government is serious about moving forward with a key component of the transition. Because it involves the divestment of assets formerly held by the state, privatization is usually considered the engine of private sector development, as it forces firms to operate in a market environment (which in itself should necessitate firm restructuring).

The speed of implementation of privatization appears to affect its outcome. That is, the faster transfer of assets, the faster the process of restructuring begins, and the more credible the government's program. Programs such as Estonia's and the Czech Republic's, which were designed and implemented quickly, seem to have been successful. At the same time, fast implementation of programs (such as Russia's) has drawn a lot of criticism for trading off apparent efficiency for equity. Latvia's and Lithuania's large-scale privatization programs have moved slowly and hence the credibility of the government's commitment to privatization has been called into question, although in Lithuania the new government did much in early 1997 to reinvigorate the process.

The privatization process also affects the rate of financial deepening and widening. First, privatization facilitates the growth of an equity market by listing shares of newly privatized firms on primary and secondary securities markets. Second, privatization in many countries has resulted in the creation of investment funds. These funds can act as mutual funds and brokerage houses; they have also become an important source of capital for investment and enterprise restructuring. In many countries where funds have operated as a part of the privatization experience, private sector growth has been rapid (the Czech Republic and Poland). Finally, including banks in the privatization (as in Poland) has also helped link privatization to financial market development. Banks have been involved in debt-for-equity swaps of firms being privatized and have participated directly in the privatization process through ownership of investment funds.

Availability of Capital

As mentioned above, limited availability of capital is perhaps a binding constraint on the development of the private sector. The ability to secure capital for restructuring or investment remains low in most transition economies and is an especially serious problem in Latvia and Lithuania. On the domestic side, the banking sector in many transition countries does not provide investment capital to firms. Lending rates are seen as excessively high,[3] perhaps due to the fact that few firms have either the collateral or a long enough history to satisfy bank lending requirements.[4] Newly privatized firms tend to face

---

[2]That is, the fast private sector development in Poland has occurred despite the slow progress of large-scale privatization.

[3]The average spread between lending and deposit rates is approximately 14 percentage points in Lithuania (March 1997) and 14 percentage points in Latvia (April 1997).

[4]See EBRD (1995), Chapter 6, for a thorough discussion of the impediments to investment in transition economies.

the problem of not having sufficient collateral and new start-up firms face both problems. On the other hand, money banks have been slow in developing their own risk assessment expertise and thus prefer to invest in safe alternatives such as domestic government securities.

Foreign direct investment (FDI) is a possible means to mitigate the capital shortage problem, but few countries have actively encouraged it. FDI is critical to private sector development because it allows the flow of both physical and human capital into a country with little adverse impact on the trade balance. In addition, FDI deployed in the export sector has a second order effect of creating new export markets.[5] Additionally, there is growing evidence that FDI acts to "prime the pump" on domestic investment as a spillover effect.[6]

Most transition economies have FDI legislation on the books, but it has taken longer for countries such as Latvia and Lithuania to harmonize other institutional foundations to facilitate FDI (such as legal codes to allow foreign participation in domestic markets). Many of the barriers to FDI are "nontangible," such as complex and nontransparent approval processes (as in Russia and Latvia) or general distrust of foreign participation in domestic markets. Estonia has been extremely successful in attracting FDI primarily due to the fact that internal (legal and institutional structures) and external policies are attractive to FDI, and Finland, its neighbor with which it shares a common cultural background and a similar language, has been investing heavily in Estonia.

In addition to the problem of augmenting the stock of capital to meet demand for investment is the issue of having access to the existing pool. That is, how easy or difficult is it for an individual entrepreneur to obtain investment capital. In many countries, notably Latvia and Lithuania, the constraint appears to apply to the ability to borrow from banks while faced with a lack of domestic equity alternatives. Apparently, Estonian entrepreneurs do not face this problem to the same degree.

Private Sector Development in the Baltics

It is difficult to generalize the experience of private sector development in the Baltics as a group.

There is a wide difference especially between Estonia on one side and Latvia and Lithuania on the other. The basis of Estonia's transition program was to open the economy to the international market (and many argue that its close ties with Finland have played a strong role in Estonia's rapid transformation), while Latvia and Lithuania have undergone economic transition more slowly—especially in the sphere of opening the economy. Estonia, for example, quickly implemented the legal and institutional frameworks necessary to support FDI, harmonizing FDI legislation with other laws (such as the commercial code). As a result, Estonia does not share the same problems that Latvia and Lithuania both face, such as delays in the establishment of a consistent set of laws and accessibility to capital.

Estonia

Private sector development in Estonia has taken place at a rapid pace. Although the EBRD estimated private sector contribution to GDP at 70 percent in 1997, that figure likely understates the true level. Estonia's rapid growth of the private sector stems from the simultaneous development of institutional infrastructure, privatization, financial deepening and widening, and encouragement of FDI.

Estonia's success in private sector development can be attributed in large part to its encouragement of both start-up firms and FDI. The EBRD estimates that approximately 15,000 new firms have been established in Estonia in the six-year period to 1997. As in Poland, the initial program concentrated on creating an economic and legal environment conducive to private sector activity. Also, as in Poland, Estonia focused its privatization program on restructuring, rather than on rapid divestment of state assets. But unlike in Poland, privatization occurred quickly perhaps because of the prominent role of foreign investment in the process.

Legal and Institutional Reform

Unlike most other transition countries, Estonia concentrated its early legal and institutional reform efforts on creating a hospitable environment for foreign investment. To that end, the government accorded foreign investors national treatment immediately after independence. Most of the legal infrastructure governing commercial activity and banking reform was adopted in 1993. It is interesting to note that bankruptcy reform was implemented in late 1992, before the adoption of the commercial code. Completion of the legal foundations for private sector development was done in 1995 and involved formalizing corporate governance mechanisms and harmonizing accounting systems to EU standards.

---

[5]Stern (1997) argues that FDI into the export sector doubly benefits the host country because foreign investors are likely to have established markets in their home country or region. Thus, in addition to the transfer of human and physical technology, a host country firm might have access to a foreign market that otherwise might be closed.

[6]See EBRD (1993), Chapter 4.3.

Privatization

Estonia's move to privatize was slower than its efforts to encourage new firm entry and FDI. The Estonian program was not implemented until mid-1993, and the goal of privatization was not simply to privatize but to bring about simultaneous restructuring. To this end, although the government implemented a voucher-based system, most large enterprises were sold via tenders based on an investor's ability to provide both capital and instill effective restructuring and governance. Despite the risk of a slow, cumbersome process, privatization moved quickly, and all large enterprises, with the exception of utilities, had been privatized by the end of 1997.

In Estonia, vouchers have not acted as a link between financial markets and privatization. Vouchers themselves are being used to purchase housing and land. Although a secondary market for vouchers was formed, the nominal value of the coupons dropped to about 18 percent of their face value as of June 1996. The reason was the lack of investment opportunities available to voucher holders.

Foreign investment and especially FDI in Estonia has been successful from the beginning of transition. The main source of foreign capital is Finland, which has linguistic and cultural ties with Estonia. In per capita terms, FDI in Estonia is approximately $295 (in 1996), by far the highest in transition economies. It has become an engine for private sector development, providing both the physical and human capital for new firms to enter markets. Also, the encouragement of FDI in privatization has helped to speed the process along and provide fresh capital for restructuring.

Availability of Capital

Estonia's banking system is still in the process of consolidation. Banks face strong competition and consequently are merging.[7] Bank restructuring began early in the transition, but it was only after successive banking crises (in 1992 and 1994) that the Bank of Estonia instituted an increasingly strong set of prudential regulations, including high minimum capital requirements. As a result, the number of operating banks has dropped. At the same time, bank credit to nongovernment entities rose by approximately 84 percent during 1997. Lending rates were approximately 12 percent on average in the fall of 1997, and deposit rates were 4 percentage points

lower. Thus, bank finance in Estonia appears to have become a viable source of domestic capital.

The formal securities market in Estonia (the Tallinn Stock Exchange) began operations in the spring of 1996, although the first financial instruments were issued and traded in early 1993. The main players on the Tallinn Stock Exchange are banks and a few new investment funds. Despite the late start of the exchange relative to other transition countries and the low number of active traders, capitalization of the exchange has grown to almost 26 percent of GDP (end-1997).

Although investment funds exist in Estonia, they rarely have become strategic investors in firms to be privatized, nor have they become active participants on the Tallinn Stock Exchange. Thus, there is little connection between privatization and equity market development. At the same time, given the fact that the Tallinn Stock Exchange has not been in operation long, the level of stock market activity is surprisingly high, approximately 26 percent of GDP at the end of 1997 (compared with the Riga Stock Exchange, which is capitalized at approximately 6.3 percent of GDP).[8] But at present, the securities market is not sectorally diverse, with most of the capital market activity concentrated in the banking sector, although the role of insurance companies is growing.

While the domestic capital market infrastructure in Estonia is thin, bank finance is possible. In part due to high levels of portfolio capital inflows, banks are able to extend credit to the private sector (i.e., the nongovernment sector). During 1997, credit to the nongovernment sector grew 84 percent in nominal terms, and in December 1997, stood at about 30 percent of GDP.[9] The demand for credit is thought to stem primarily from the growth in the number of new firms.

Latvia

Due to the slow pace of structural reform, which has inhibited both privatization and the creation of new firms, Latvia's private sector development has been concentrated mainly in small service sector enterprises or retail shops. Thus if the growth of the private sector is viewed as an index of development,

---

[7]From 1992 to 1995, the number of banks dropped from 42 to 21, and from 1995 to the end of 1997, the number dropped to 11. Data from the Bank of Estonia, *Eesti Pank Bulletin,* No. 4 (Tallinn, 1996).

[8]Stock market capitalization refers to the market value of the shares listed.

[9]The comparable figure for Latvia was 7 percent of GDP. The figure for both countries was calculated by using the level of domestic credit in nongovernment sectors. In Latvia, the figure includes domestic credit to enterprises, most of which are still state owned. It should be noted that the growth rate of credit to the nongovernment sector in Estonia began to slow down toward the end of 1997 in response to monetary and prudential measures taken by the Bank of Estonia.

the seemingly high level of private sector contribution to GDP (the EBRD estimates the level at 65 percent in 1997) might be an overstatement. Since January 1996, however, Latvia has worked quickly to remove remaining barriers to the growth of the private sector.

Legal and Institutional Framework

Despite the fact that Latvia began the transition in 1992, it has taken about four years to adopt more thorough legislative and institutional frameworks necessary for private sector development. Although basic legislation was completed by 1994, the legal framework surrounding privatization, FDI, and capital market development was not completed until 1996. The incomplete legislation led to two discernible problems. First, programs such as privatization have taken much longer to complete than expected. Second, the long process resulted in the persistence of government participation in markets, with possible distortions and other adverse effects on private sector growth.

Privatization

The result of the various privatization programs as of the end of 1997 is that less than ½ of 1 percent of large enterprises has actually been privatized. Latvia has now entered the second phase of privatization, which began with a series of laws adopted in 1996 to eliminate the problems experienced during the first phase by speeding up the process and attracting foreign participation. To date, nearly 1,300 units have been approved for privatization, half of which have signed sales agreements. Second, changes in liquidation procedures now allow for liquidated firms to be sold either as one unit or in pieces, which should accelerate the process. Next, the ability to buy land both under privatized enterprises and as an asset in itself was formalized, and a law extending the right of land ownership to foreigners has been prepared and will shortly be considered by the parliament.[10] Moreover, nearly all sectors have been opened to foreign participation in privatization.[11] Additionally, foreign investors were granted the right to purchase vouchers, allowing them to participate directly in privatization.

Despite positive legislative changes, such as the removal of restrictions on foreign participation in both asset and land privatization and the opening of most sectors to any potential buyer, privatization in Latvia still faces informal obstacles. One strong impediment in large-scale privatization is the process itself. The approval process is long and complicated. With each level in the process, there is an opportunity to slow down or even stop privatization. While these problems might have stemmed more from a lack of political will than from explicit barriers, the process itself allows for these informal obstacles that can prove to be more formidable than the explicit barriers. For privatization to move more quickly, there must be a commitment on the part of all parties involved to accelerate the procedure by both streamlining it and eliminating the informal barriers.

Availability of Capital

In banking, credit to private enterprises has fallen from 16 percent to 10 percent of GDP from the period of the banking crisis (June 1995) to the end of 1997. This decline in credit is attributed to the fallout of the banking crisis. That is, the number of operative banks has declined steadily this year to 33 (only 19 of which can accept deposits), as a result of the implementation of strong prudential banking regulations and banking supervision in the aftermath of the banking crisis. For example, the minimum capital requirement for banks has been raised from LVL 100,000 to LVL 2 million as of April 1998. Interest rates on loans are currently low, dropping from 34 percent at the end of 1995 to 12 percent as of the end of 1997; deposit rates have dropped to approximately 5.0 percent (three-month maturity), which is still negative in real terms. The narrowing of interest rate spreads is a strong, positive signal of financial market health.

Perhaps the most serious constraint on obtaining bank finance is the scarcity of usable collateral for new start-up firms. Doubts about the viability of newly privatized firms that do not have collateral make it difficult for banks to lend, though this constraint is being reduced by land registration (one means of providing collateral). In Latvia, land registration has moved slowly, with only 25 percent of all land registered as of the end of 1997.[12] Two reasons are usually cited for the slow pace: high cost and large time investment to complete the process. Estimates of the cost of registering land range from the official cost (LVL 30) to reported actual costs of

---

[10]The existing law restricts a foreign investor who wishes to purchase the land under a privatized enterprise to hold not more than 49 percent equity in the privatized firm.

[11]Only a few sectors remain closed to foreign investors such as those pertaining to national security. Foreigners can now buy land except in a ten kilometer radius of the frontier.

---

[12]The government envisaged that by the end of 1996, 20 percent of all land would be registered and by the end of 1997, 30 percent.

LVL 280–300 (approximately $600). Most enterprises are on multiple units of land, which makes the process even more expensive. Moreover, the process of registration, which includes getting all the necessary approvals could take from six months to one year to complete. Finally, land owners fear that registration will increase their tax burden because land is a taxable asset.

On the securities side, the Riga Stock Exchange is growing rapidly, primarily due to the increasing number of newly privatized enterprises.[13] The creation of a Securities Market Commission has also facilitated faster growth of the market and should strengthen investor confidence. In addition, there are currently no start-up firms listed on the Riga exchange, primarily due to the fact that most of them are small and would generate little demand for their shares. The future growth of the exchange to a large extent depends on the rate of privatization. The Riga Stock Exchange expects that capitalization will exceed 30 percent of GDP when large-scale privatization is completed.

FDI in Latvia has increased since 1992 but remains low in comparison with other transition countries. EBRD estimates that the level of FDI per capita in Latvia was $85 in 1997. Until 1996, there were many formal restrictions to FDI, ranging from exclusion of direct foreign participation in privatization to severe constraints on which sectors could receive FDI. Most of the legal restrictions were eliminated in 1996, and the Government's commitment to attracting FDI appears strong.

Lithuania

Despite the figures reported in Section II, private sector development in Lithuania is still in its beginning stages. Most of the private sector activity is in the service sector, with the share of private enterprises in manufacturing still small. The sluggish pace of private sector development in Lithuania can be attributed to the slow rate of institutional reform, especially in the area of legal reform and privatization, as well as the constraints on investment capital.

Legal and Institutional Framework

Perhaps the most formidable impediment to private sector development in Lithuania currently is the state of legal and institutional reform. The EBRD reports that the competition policy governing enterprise activity in the market has contradictory statutes. Thus the "rules of the game" for new enterprises to enter and compete are not clear. On the investment side, there are still few laws regulating investment and securities markets, and those laws that exist are unclear and impose conflicting requirements. In some cases, the law is transparent but is difficult to use in practice. For example, there is a bankruptcy law (approved in early 1997, to replace an earlier law judged to have been highly ineffective) that in itself is sound and consistent with a market-based economy, but implementation in the court system is being delayed owing to lack of legal expertise and court capacity. Further, investors complain that the laws that are currently on the books are not well adapted to local needs. Finally, information about changes are typically not published, adding to uncertainty.[14]

Privatization

As of mid–1996, approximately 30 percent of medium- and large-scale enterprises have been transferred into private hands.[15] Though the number of large-scale enterprises privatized suggests that privatization has moved decisively forward, it should be noted that the initial privatization program (voucher-based) has been in place since 1991, and the second and more comprehensive program (cash-based, approved in 1995) is now under way after many delays. In early 1997, the new government gave a significant boost to the privatization process by announcing the sale (via international tenders) of 14 of the largest enterprises in the energy, transport, and telecommunications sectors. In addition, the government also initially reduced by 50 percent the number of enterprises excluded from privatization until the year 2000 and, by year-end, eliminated the so-called negative lists altogether, except for a narrowly defined set of enterprises in which state participation is seen to be inevitable (e.g., the Ignalina Nuclear Power Station).

Availability of Capital

The availability of domestic bank finance to entrepreneurs is low, due to the sharp contraction of the

---

[13]The Riga Stock Exchange began trading on July 25, 1995 and currently lists 28 companies, Unibanka (which constitutes 75 percent of the trading volume), and Riga Transportation Fleet (3 percent), while adding treasury bill quotations (7 percent), mortgage notes (13 percent), and other listings (2 percent). Total capitalization of the market is LVL 200 million, approximately 6.3 percent of GDP. The level of turnover on the Riga Stock Exchange has been falling since its peak earlier in 1996. This is compared with the Czech Republic, in which the Prague Stock Exchange is capitalized to about 50 percent of GDP. Latvia source: Baltic News Service; Czech source: Lieberman and others (1995), p. 36.

[14]See EBRD (1995), p. 112.

[15]EBRD (1996), p. 161.

banking sector following the 1995 crisis. Lithuania's current banking system is concentrated in three state-majority-owned commercial banks (the State Savings Bank, the State Agricultural Bank, and the State Commercial Bank). State-controlled banks effectively account for 50 percent of all deposits in the banking system.

The contraction of the banking sector as a result of the crisis and implementation of stricter prudential regulations at the beginning of 1996 should provide a more solid banking system that, perhaps in the medium term, will provide capital. In the aftermath of the crisis, banks were wary of lending to the private sector, as can be inferred from the contraction of credit to the private sector in 1996,[16] but a process of recovery was in evidence in 1997 when a sharp recovery of private sector credit supported real GDP growth on the order of 6 percent.

On the securities side, there has been little activity, and hence the ability to raise capital through equity offerings remains small. To date, the National Stock Exchange (which began operations in 1993) lists 400 firms, and its level of capitalization is about 18 percent of GDP as of the end of 1997. The relatively small size of the equity market can be attributed to the slow pace of privatization.

Foreign direct investment into Lithuania has not yet been a primary source of investment funds. The EBRD estimates per capita FDI at $41 in 1996. While there are no legal impediments to FDI (profits can be repatriated freely, and there are no formal restrictions), the combination of a nontransparent legal system, slow pace of privatization (as well as some restrictions on foreign participation), and underdevelopment of domestic capital markets (resulting in difficulties in local co-financing) have all contributed, at least until 1997, to a low level of FDI. In addition, the lack of experience with foreign investment has resulted in a mistrust of foreign participation in domestic markets, which is manifested in the slow approval process.

Limited access to capital in Lithuania is a direct result of the banking sector being in a process of consolidation, still relatively low levels of FDI, and the lack of collateralizable assets. At present, no system exists for registering ownership interests or pledges of assets to be used as collateral against loans. Since the banking crisis and stricter prudential regulations, banks are more wary of lending, and the lack of a formal mechanism for providing collateral raises the risk premium, again manifested in relatively high lending rates.

---

[16]Credit to the nongovernment sector contracted in nominal terms by approximately 5 percent between the third quarter of 1995 and the same period of 1996.

Policies and Program Design to Remove Obstacles to Private Sector Development

For the private sector to develop, it is important that the economic environment be conducive to firm entry and exit, investment, and competition. Promoting such an environment would involve:

- establishing a solid legal infrastructure, comprehensive enough that it covers all areas of private sector development as a basic step in the process;
- ensuring the rapid completion of privatization programs once they are under way;
- establishing linkages between privatization and capital market development (through investment funds);
- encouraging FDI involvement in privatization to accelerate the process, as well as facilitate simultaneous enterprise restructuring;
- promoting FDI, given capital market constraints; and
- developing domestic capital markets, given that the single most binding constraint on private sector development is the shortage of capital.

Conclusions

Private sector development is an important component of economic transition. The level of private sector development can be thought of as a measure of economic reform. In the long run, private sector development is needed to put an economy on a sustained growth path. The issue is especially important for the Baltics, where the "first stage of transition" has largely come to an end and structural obstacles are becoming the most serious impediment to economic growth. The experience of the Baltic countries shows how formidable the impediments to private sector development can be even if macroeconomic policy is sound.

First, the establishment of a solid legal infrastructure is a basic condition for private sector development. As both Latvia and Lithuania have found, without an adequate legal framework to support the other main areas of private sector development (privatization, domestic capital market development, and foreign investment), it will be difficult for the private sector to grow, given both distortions in the market and lack of knowledge of "the rules of the game."

Second, the varied experiences of the sequencing of privatization suggest that privatization itself need not be the first item on the transition agenda as long as the legal and economic environments are conducive to the entry of start-up firms (as in Poland and Estonia). Once privatization begins, however, it is important that it be completed quickly to enhance credibility, with due regard for rule of law and good governance considerations. Thus, as long as the private sector grows, it is less important if the source of growth is privatization or new firm entry as long as both take place. The psychological importance of privatization carried out in a context of respect for the law should not be underestimated. Though the tangible results may or may not catalyze private sector development, depending on the individual conditions in each country, the fact that the process is moving ahead is a sign of governmental commitment to developing a private sector. That is, if residents see that privatization is happening quickly, it might shape expectations that transition is progressing and is irreversible. In many transition countries, changing expectations is a necessary condition to stimulating private sector development. Once an economy is privatized, it becomes increasingly difficult to reverse private sector development. Thus both domestic and foreign investors perceive the economic risk of policy reversal as minimized.

Third, all of the above country experiences suggest that the fastest, most efficient means of developing the capital market is to encourage linkages between privatization and the equity market via the use of investment funds. The funds themselves can be a catalyst for equity trading, providing both the volume of shares and continued activity in the market. Countries that have not encouraged the use of investment funds tend to have a more rudimentary equity market system. Because transition countries need financial widening (and deepening) and because many transition economy banking systems are not extending much credit, it is imperative that alternative forms of intermediation be developed.

Similarly, participation of foreign investors in the privatization process (as in Estonia and Poland) can be a catalyst for private sector development because it provides additional human and physical capital. Given the severe shortage of capital facing most private entrepreneurs, FDI is one means of alleviating this constraint. Further, FDI will increase the possibility of fast and effective restructuring and installation of good governance mechanisms.

Finally, alleviating the constraint on capital means that domestic capital markets must be widened and deepened. This reform must start with the banking system and involves allowing insolvent banks to fail and recapitalizing potentially solvent banks. Additionally, sound fiscal and monetary policies are necessary for the emergence of an appropriate structure of lending and deposit rates. And, equity market and alternative instruments should be developed through the adoption of appropriate government legislation, a stable economic environment, privatization, and foreign investment.

References

Bank of Estonia, *Eesti Park Bulletin,* various issues.

Central Statistical Bureau of Latvia and Latvian Privatization Agency, 1996, "Privatization Process in Latvia," *Quarterly Bulletin* (Riga, various issues).

Diamond, Douglas, 1984, "Financial Intermediation and Delegated Monitoring," *Review of Economic Studies,* Vol. 51, pp. 393–414.

Dornbusch, Rudiger, and Alejandro Reynuso, 1989, "Financial Factors in Economic Development," NBER Working Paper 2889 (Cambridge, Massachusetts: National Bureau of Economic Research, March).

European Bank for Reconstruction and Development, 1993, *Annual Economic Outlook* (London, September).

———, 1994, 1995, 1996, *Transition Report* (London, September).

———, 1996, *Transition Report—Update* (London, April).

Estrin, Saul, ed., 1994, *Privatization in Central and Eastern Europe* (London: Longman Press).

Fazzari, Steven M., R. Glen Hubbard, and Bruce C. Peterson, 1988, "Financing Constraints and Corporate Investment," *Brookings Papers on Economic Activity: 1,* pp. 141–203.

Fry, Maxwell, 1982, "Models of Financially Repressed Developing Economies," *World Development,* Vol. 10, pp. 731–50.

Frydman, Roman, Andrej Rapaczynski, and John S. Earle, and others, 1993, 1994, *The Privatization Process in Central Europe,* Vols. 1 and 2 (London: Central European University Press).

Gertler, Mark, 1988, "Financial Structure and Aggregate Economic Activity," NBER Working Paper 2559 (Cambridge, Massachusetts: National Bureau of Economic Research).

———, R. Glen Hubbard, and Anil Kashyap, 1990, "Interest Rate Spreads, Credit Constraints, and Investment Fluctuations: An Empirical Investigation," NBER Working Paper 3495 (Cambridge, Massachusetts: National Bureau of Economic Research, October).

Kopint-Datorg, 1995, *Privatization in the Transition Process: Recent Experiences in Eastern Europe* (New York: United Nations).

Lankes, Hans-Peter, and A.J. Venables, 1996, *"Foreign Direct Investment in Eastern Europe and the Former Soviet Union: Results from a Survey of Investors"* (draft; European Bank for Reconstruction and Development, April).

Lieberman, Ira W., and others, 1995, *"Mass Privatization in Central and Eastern Europe and the Former Soviet Union,"* World Bank Studies of Economies in Transformation Number 16 (Washington: World Bank, June).

Murphy, Kevin, Andrei Schleifer, and Robert Vishny, 1989, "The Big Push," *Journal of Political Economy,* Vol. 97 (October) pp. 1003–1026.

Republic of Latvia, Ministry of Economy, 1996, *Economic Development of Latvia* (Riga, June).

Stern, Richard E., 1992, "Financial Market Efficiency, Increasing Returns, and Economic Growth in Post-Socialist Economies" (Ph.D. dissertation; University of California at Berkeley, September).

———, 1994, "Fundamentals of the Financial Market in the Czech Republic and Its Implications for Corporate Governance," paper presented at the 1994 Annual Meetings of the American Economic Association (Boston, January).

———, 1996, "Policy Analysis of Foreign Direct Investment in the Russian Federation: A Study of the Current State Affairs and Prospects for the Future" Institute for Hohre Studien Working Paper 34 (Vienna, January).

———, 1997, *Impediments to Exports,* ed. by Janos Gacs and Richard Cooper (London: Edward Elgar Press).

Stiglitz, Joseph E., 1991, "Government, Financial Markets, and Economic Development," NBER Working Paper 3669 (Cambridge, Massachusetts: National Bureau of Economic Research, April).

VII The Baltic Countries and Accession to the European Union

Ann-Margret Westin

Since 1993, the relationships between the European Union and the three Baltic countries, Estonia, Latvia, and Lithuania, have deepened through a variety of agreements aimed at further developing economic and political relations and, ultimately, integration with the EU. The most important agreements have been the Agreements on Trade and Commercial and Economic Cooperation, which came into force in February and March 1993; the Free Trade Agreements, which came into force on January 1, 1995; and the Association, or Europe Agreements, which were signed in June 1995 and came into force in February 1998. Through these Agreements, the Baltics asserted their intentions to become fully integrated with the EU. They formally applied for EU membership in the fall of 1995.

Pre-Accession Strategy for the Associated Countries of Central and Eastern Europe—the Baltics

At the Copenhagen summit in 1993, it was decided "that the associated countries in Central and Eastern Europe that so desire shall become members of the European Union. Accession will take place as soon as an associated country is able to assume the obligations of membership by satisfying the economic and political conditions required."[1] At the same time, the economic and political conditions that had to be fulfilled for membership were also defined. The following year, at the Essen summit in December 1994, it was confirmed that the countries of central Europe could become members in the EU, and the Union's accession policy was refocused toward these countries in light of their future membership. In particular, a "pre-accession strategy" was determined, which outlined the means through which the Union would assist the associated countries in their integration. The strategy, which was tailored to

meet the needs of those countries with which Europe Agreements had been concluded or would be concluded in the near future, encompasses the following: the Association Agreements, whereby the EU offers associated countries the trade concessions and other benefits that are normally affiliated with full membership; the creation of a "structured dialogue," which provides a framework through which associated countries and member states can discuss issues of common concern; financial grants, policy advice, and training through the Phare Program; and a White Paper on "legislation harmonization." A list of the Association Agreements signed between the EU and central and eastern European countries and the formal membership applications submitted is provided in Table 7.1. As noted in the table, while the Association Agreements of the Baltic countries just recently came into effect, that of Slovenia, the last one to be signed, is still being ratified. Reviewed below are the general accession conditions and the pre-accession strategy for EU membership that apply to the associated countries of central and eastern Europe and their relevance for the three Baltic countries, and the possible timetable for accession negotiations and, ultimately, EU membership.

Admission Criteria

At the 1993 Copenhagen summit, the European Council listed the economic and political conditions that the associated countries in central and eastern Europe would have to satisfy to become members of the EU. These criteria were (1) stability of institutions guaranteeing democracy, the rule of law, human rights, and respect for the protection of minorities; (2) the existence of a functioning market economy and the capacity to cope with competitive pressures and market forces within the EU; and (3) the ability to take on the obligations of membership, including adherence to the aims of political, economic, and monetary union. A fourth precondition was subsequently added, stating that the EU itself should show that it had the capacity to handle new members without slowing the momentum of the European integration process.

---

[1]See Commission of the European Communities (1994a, p.1) and also (1994b, 1995b, and 1996f).

Table 7.1. Association Agreements and EU Membership Applications of Central and Eastern European Countries

Country	Association Agreement Signed	Association Agreement Came into Force	Official Application for EU Membership
Bulgaria	March 1993	February 1995	December 1995
Czech Republic	October 1993	February 1995	January 1996
Estonia	June 1995	February 1998	November 1995
Hungary	December 1991	February 1994	March 1994
Latvia	June 1995	February 1998	October 1995
Lithuania	June 1995	February 1998	December 1995
Poland	December 1991	February 1994	April 1994
Romania	February 1993	February 1995	June 1995
Slovakia	October 1993	February 1995	June 1995
Slovenia	June 1996	—[1]	June 1996

Source: Commission of the European Communities.
[1]Still being ratified.

The criteria set by the European Council were very general and failed to provide any concrete definitions or guidelines on what exactly would be required of the associated countries. Therefore, during the Copenhagen summit, France made a proposal (known as the "French list") including a more detailed description of the admission criteria. According to the list, the general state of development of the economy could be measured in terms of GDP per capita while the functioning of the market economy could be measured by the extent of privatization. It was also suggested that the criteria should include a demonstrated ability to deliver a quantifiable level of social protection, as well as control of public debt and inflation. Furthermore, it should be possible to assess the country's monetary and fiscal policies, including convertibility and stability of the local currency and policies on capital movements. There should be an efficient banking system. Also, the economy's degree of openness should be measurable in terms of the proportion of external trade in GDP and the impact of the country's economy on that of the Union. Finally, the capacity of national administrations to implement domestic and EU laws as well as the existence of a modern fiscal system should be included in the assessment of economic health.

Pre-Accession Strategy

Association (Europe) Agreements

The Europe Agreements are the most wide-ranging agreements that the EU has ever entered into. They cover political dialogue and economic integration as well as cultural and financial cooperation and are concluded for unlimited periods. The first Europe Agreements between the EU and central European countries were signed as early as 1991 but the agreements acquired greater political significance following the 1993 Copenhagen summit where EU membership of the associated countries was recognized as an objective shared by the EU. All countries that sign Europe Agreements become eligible for membership and, since the agreement on the pre-accession strategy at the 1994 Essen summit, these Agreements have become the main element of the framework within which countries work toward EU membership.[2] A key element of the Europe Agreements is the series of bilateral meetings between the EU and each of the potential members, concerning, inter alia, the implementation of the pre-accession strategy and intraregional cooperation. The pre-accession strategy also introduces a number of measures to promote trade for the partner countries, and the Europe Agreements aim at gradually establishing free trade in industrial products over the transition period on an asymmetric basis: the EU, as the stronger economic partner, opens it markets more rapidly than the associated country.

The Europe Agreements signed between the EU and the three Baltic countries in June 1995 have since been ratified by the parliaments of the EU member countries and by the EU itself. The agreements came into effect in February 1998 and now

___

[2]In addition to the Europe Agreements signed between the EU and the ten countries of central and eastern Europe, EU Association Agreements with Malta and Cyprus came into force already in 1971 and 1973, respectively. See Commission of the European Communities (1993a and 1993b).

fully supplant the previous trade and cooperation agreements; they also provide a political dialogue between the EU and the Baltic countries and include provisions on matters such as the establishment of firms, movement of workers and capital, supply of services, economic, cultural, and financial cooperation, and cooperation on prevention of illegal activities.

The general principles governing the three Baltic Agreements are more or less the same, with one important exception in that Latvia and Lithuania enjoy a transitional period, ending December 31, 1999, in the areas of trade liberalization and competition.[3] No transitional period was provided for Estonia in light of the country's economic openness toward the rest of the world. In the framework of the Estonian Association Agreement, a free trade area was established between Estonia and the EU as of January 1, 1995, and no efforts to abolish supports and restrictions contradicting EU rules will be necessary. In Latvia, it has been agreed to gradually establish a free trade area with the EU over a transitional period starting January 1, 1995 and lasting a maximum of four years. The governing principles are those of the Association Agreement as well as those of the World Trade Organization and the "New" General Agreements on Tariffs and Trade (GATT) of 1994. Also, most of the few remaining export duties are to be abolished by the end of 1998 at the latest. Meanwhile, in Lithuania, remaining custom duties on exports and imports vis-à-vis the EU are to be abolished by January 1, 2001. In Latvia and Lithuania, all quantitative restrictions on imports and exports vis-à-vis the EU were abolished on January 1, 1995. Also, the EU, Latvia, and Lithuania have each declared their readiness to reduce custom duties more rapidly if the economic situation permits.

Structured Dialogue

At the Copenhagen summit, the EU agreed on a multilateral framework of regular joint meetings at the ministerial level between the Union and the associated countries. The structured dialogue provides a framework for the discussion of issues of common concern, including the Common Foreign and Security Policy and justice and interior issues. It also familiarizes prospective member countries with the EU's decision-making process and institutional setup. Since 1995, government leaders and EU ministers have been meeting their counterparts from the associated countries, including the Baltics, at regular intervals. Twice a year, heads of state and government have met during the European Council; foreign

affairs ministers and ministers responsible for justice and interior affairs have also convened twice a year.

Phare Program

The Phare Program, which initially was developed as an immediate response to the structural challenges facing central and eastern European countries, has become one of the cornerstones of the pre-accession strategy.[4] The program provides grants as well as policy advice and training to support partner countries through the process of economic transformation and strengthening of democracy. Through research studies, capital grants, guarantee schemes, and credit lines, the program acts as a catalyst by unlocking funds for important projects from other donors, but it also invests directly in infrastructure together with international financing institutions. The program has been implemented in cooperation with other international institutions to ensure consistency in policy and sector strategy and to avoid duplication of efforts; in fact, the Phare Program has worked closely with, and has provided know-how, training, and support to the IMF, the World Bank, and the European Bank for Reconstruction and Development. The Phare budget is determined by the European Parliament and the Council of the EU, and after six years of operation (1990–95), a total of ECU 5.4 billion has been made available to 11 partner countries.[5] Funds through the Phare Program are allocated both to national and multicountry programs, with the latter most prevalent in the areas of environment, energy, transportation, nuclear safety, customs, and the fight against illegal drug trade.[6]

The Baltic countries have been part of the Phare Program since 1992 and have received assistance through both national and multicountry programs.[7] Between 1992 and 1995, the three Baltic countries received a total of ECU 289.5 million, covering the provision of technical assistance, financial assistance (small and medium-sized firm credit lines), training, and limited supplies of equipment. In all three countries, the programs initially focused on macroeco-

---

[3]See Pautola (1996)

[4]PHARE, which now encompasses all the central and eastern European associated member countries, is an acronym for "Poland and Hungary: Aid for Restructuring of Economies."

[5]In addition to the ten central and eastern European countries with which the EU has signed Europe Agreements, the Phare Program also includes Albania.

[6]See Commission of the European Communities (1996d and 1996e).

[7]In addition, the Baltics received ECU 15 million in 1991 through the TACIS ("Technical Assistance to the Commonwealth of Independent States") program which was designed to promote the development of the newly independent states of the former Soviet Union.

nomic stabilization and restructuring, including privatization, industrial restructuring, and financial sector development. The program for Estonia also included a number of strategy studies in the areas of energy, environment, and transportation, and in Lithuania, Phare funding was also used for the preparation of three large-scale studies in the areas of agriculture, transport, and energy.

Since 1995, the EU has prepared Multi-Annual Indicative Programs (MIPs) for the Baltic countries covering a total estimated allocation of ECU 430 million for the 1995–99 period. These programs are more concentrated in character and will focus on pre-accession preparations (including the implementation of Free Trade and Europe Agreements and the adoption of the internal market's *acquis communautaire*); medium-term restructuring (poststabilization economic development); infrastructure investment; and regional cooperation. The exact implementation of the MIPs differs among the three countries, with Estonia placing further emphasis on export development and public sector management while private sector development, agriculture, social sector and human resources development are receiving more attention in Latvia and Lithuania.

White Paper on Approximation of Laws

Within the framework of the Europe Agreements, the associated countries have begun approximating their legislative frameworks to move toward the economic freedoms that constitute the basis of the EU's internal market. Given the magnitude and complexity of this task, the European Council endorsed a White Paper in Cannes in June 1995 to help the countries prepare as rapidly and efficiently as possible.[8] The White Paper sets out the body of essential internal market legislation divided into 23 sectors. These sectors cover, inter alia, the free movement of capital and persons, competition policy, social policy, agriculture, transportation, the environment, telecommunications, direct and indirect taxation, public procurement, financial services, energy, and consumer protection.

The Baltic countries generally face the greatest challenges in the areas of company legislation and contract enforcement; laws relating to the operation of the financial system; the protection of intellectual property rights; and competition policies. To create a secure and predictable environment in which companies can operate, national laws will need to be harmonized across Europe so that obstacles to a company's freedom to establish operations are removed and an equivalent degree of protection is provided

throughout the Community. The development of the financial sector will be another key issue for the successful transition of the Baltic countries, requiring not only the existence of the basic legislative environment but also laws regulating the issuance and ownership of securities as well as the existence of regulated markets where securities are issued and traded. Enhanced intellectual property rights will also be important to ensure the proper incentives for innovation, research, and development. A final key challenge for the Baltics will be to improve their competition policies, one of the cornerstones for the creation of an internal market and a precondition for EU accession.

Timetable

Throughout the process, the Baltic countries have been insisting on exact timetables and on the importance of each country being dealt with separately, according to its own merits. In particular, during 1996 and the first half of 1997, Estonia argued repeatedly that the economic achievement of a country and not its geopolitical aspects must take priority in the admission of new members into the EU, and that, consequently, the economic success of Estonia should imply that it would be included in the first wave of EU enlargement (see below). Meanwhile, the EU has been reluctant to pin down any guarantees or commitments, indicating that it would be premature to offer an exact timetable at this stage. Furthermore, while the EU has stated a preference for dealing with the Baltics as a single entity, differences in the pace of the transition process and implementation of economic and political reforms among the three countries implied that the EU would have to treat each applicant more or less on an individual basis.

In their endeavor to become members of the EU, the focus of the associated countries of central and eastern Europe has been on the outcome of the Intergovernmental Conference (IGC), a conference of representatives of the governments of the EU member states. One of the main tasks of the IGC, which got under way in March of 1996, was to decide on the eastern enlargement of the EU, a process that includes a major review of the current institutions and decision-making procedures of the EU. In the end, the outcome of the Intergovernmental Conference, together with the economic development and legal progress of the associated countries, had a decisive influence on the time frame and conditions of the membership negotiations.

To determine with which associated countries to initiate the first wave of membership negotiations for its eastern enlargement, the EU asked all prospective members in central and eastern Europe to fill out an extensive questionnaire; the 300,000 pages of an-

---

[8]See Commission of the European Communities (1995a)..

swers by the associated nations were subsequently examined by the EU ahead of the June 1997 Amsterdam summit. Following the summit, the European Commission presented a package known as "Agenda 2000," comprising four key sets of documents on enlargement, which set out (1) the Commission's view on individual countries' applications; (2) an evaluation of the impact of enlargement on EU policies, notably on the Common Agricultural Policy and the regional funds; (3) a draft budget to run from 2000 taking into account the prospect of enlargement; and (4) a composite paper bringing together the Commission's overall analysis of the applicant's readiness for membership and the likely impact on the EU.[9] In particular, the Commission recommended that the central and eastern European associated member countries to be included in the first wave of membership negotiations should be, in alphabetical order, the Czech Republic, Estonia, Hungary, Poland, and Slovenia; in addition, it was recommended that membership negotiations also be initiated with Cyprus.

A final decision regarding the timetable of the Eastern enlargement was taken at the EU Luxembourg summit in December last year, indicating that while full accession talks, that is, bilateral negotiations at the government level, will be initiated in April this year with the six countries suggested by the European Commission, preparatory talks will begin at the same time with the remaining central and eastern European applicant countries, that is, Bulgaria, Latvia, Lithuania, Romania, and Slovakia. The enlargement process will officially begin on March 30, 1998, with a meeting of foreign ministers from the 15 EU member nations and from the 11 applicant countries. All 11 countries will be offered "pre-accession partnerships," including financial aid and annual reviews to determine whether new countries should join the negotiations. The six "first wave" countries will also be invited to an intergovernmental conference, with the eventual aim of signing accession agreements; actual EU membership for the first associated member countries is, however, not expected to take place until 2002 at the earliest, and most likely not until 2004–05.[10]

As mentioned, the exact timing of EU accession for the three Baltic countries will in the end depend on both the EU's willingness and capacity to absorb new members and the status of the economic, political, social, and legal reform processes in the three countries. In that context, it is worthwhile noting that while the White Paper is encouraging in its detailed

step-by-step advice, it clearly highlights the enormous amount of work yet to be completed. The EU legal framework needs to be translated into each country's own language and domestic laws need to be approximated to EU legislation.[11] The next section will review the EU accession criteria as well as the Maastricht criteria for participation in the European Monetary Union (EMU) and the status of the Baltic countries in this regard, examining both the progress achieved so far as well as the areas where further measures will be needed.

EU Membership and Implications for Economic Policy in the Baltics

With the Baltics still in transition, and with their economic, political, and social systems still forming, the terms of admission into the EU and the problem of defining the admission criteria have become contentious. This section will review the economic and sociopolitical situation of the Baltic countries, both regarding progress made in the last years toward meeting the EU accession criteria and areas in which further efforts are still needed. Progress will be discussed both in terms of a number of "transition" indicators as defined by the EBRD and in terms of the socioeconomic variables included in the "French" list of admission criteria. Furthermore, having entered the EU, the subsequent question for the Baltics will be adherence to the Maastricht criteria and the timing of EMU participation. Therefore, the Baltics' current performance vis-à-vis the Maastricht convergence criteria on inflation, state finances, long-term interest rates, and exchange rate stability, and the outlook for eventual Baltic EMU participation are also reviewed.

The Baltics in Transition: EBRD Indicators

In its Transition Reports, the EBRD points out that when discussing the progress made by transition countries in their transformation toward a market economy, "one of the most important lessons is that there can be, and have been, different paths to a market economy, just as there are many forms of the market economy itself."[12] However, at the same time, it acknowledges that "there are important common features of well-functioning market economies and of effective transitions." Therefore, since 1994,

---

[9]See Commission of the European Communities (1997b).

[10]See, for example, Backé (1997) for a discussion on the first wave of eastern EU enlargement.

[11]For example, some 400 directives reportedly must be introduced before the end of 1999 to align Latvian legislation with the EU standards while, as of mid-1997, Estonia's laws still needed to be aligned with at least 1,000 EU directives, an undertaking that is estimated to cost some EEK 400 million.

[12]EBRD (1996), p. 2.

the EBRD has published a number of indicators of progress in market-oriented reform for 25 countries in central and eastern Europe, the Baltics, Russia, and the other countries of the former Soviet Union.[13] The indicators try to capture progress in the areas of enterprises, markets and trade, financial institutions, and legal reform. While they cannot capture all dimensions of the transition process, they provide an overview of the relative stages of transition of the different countries. The 1994–97 EBRD transition indicators are presented for the three Baltic countries in Table 7.2. As can be seen from the table, the indicators overlap with some of the measures in the "French" list, including the extent of privatization, the existence of a well-functioning banking system, and the capacity to implement legal reform. The numbers assigned to each indicator represent the general level of transition achieved in a certain area, as assessed by the EBRD, with most advanced industrial economies qualifying for the 4+ rating for most of the indicators (the definitions for the EBRD transition indicators are provided in Table 7.3). While the indicators are meant primarily to assess the status of reform rather than the pace of change itself,[14] Table 7.2 also illustrates the progress achieved

in the Baltics since 1994. According to the EBRD, the three Baltic countries have now all reached "advanced" stages of transition, in contrast to many of the other transition countries, which still remain at early or intermediate stages of transition.[15]

During the 1994–97 period, all three Baltic countries have made progress in privatization. Latvia has been the slowest of the three in large-scale privatization; while only a few of the large state-owned enterprises in Latvia have been privatized, about 30 percent of Lithuania's and virtually all of the medium-sized and large enterprises included in Estonia's 1993–95 privatization program have been privatized. In 1997, Lithuania announced the privatization (through international tenders) of 14 of the largest enterprises in the energy, telecommunications, and transport services. Small companies have been almost completely privatized in the Baltic countries, with Estonia reaching an "industrial-country rating" in this area in 1996; meanwhile, sales of land and real estate remain more problematic. Estonia and Lithuania now have private sector shares of GDP of some 70 percent compared with an estimated 60 percent share for Latvia.[16]

---

[13]See EBRD (1997).

[14]For instance, Slovenia's 4+ rating on small-scale privatization despite the lack of a comprehensive privatization program reflects the fact that small-scale activity in Slovenia was largely private before the transition began.

[15]Similarly, Croatia, the Czech Republic, Hungary, Poland, the Slovak Republic, and Slovenia, that is, the majority of the associated EU member countries of central and eastern Europe, are classified as advanced transition countries.

[16]By comparison, on average more than 75 percent of enterprises in advanced industrial countries are in private hands.

Table 7.2. EBRD Transition Indicators[1]

	Estonia				Latvia				Lithuania			
	1994	1995	1996	1997	1994	1995	1996	1997	1994	1995	1996	1997
Private sector share of GDP in percent (midyear estimate)	55	65	70	70	55	60	60	60	50	55	65	70
Large-scale privatization	3	4	4	4	2	2	3	3	3	3	3	3
Small-scale privatization	4	4	4+	4+	3	4	4	4	4	4	4	4
Enterprise restructuring[2]	3	3	3	3	2	2	3	3–	2	2	3	3–
Price liberalization[3]	3	3	3	3	3	3	3	3	3	3	3	3
Trade and foreign exchange system	4	4	4	4	4	4	4	4	4	4	4	4
Competition policy	n.a.	3	3	3–	n.a.	2	2	3–	n.a.	2	2	2+
Banking reform and interest rate liberalization	3	3	3	3+	3	3	3	3	2	3	3	3
Securities markets and nonbank financial institutions	n.a.	2	2	3	n.a.	2	2	2+	n.a.	2	2	2+
Extensiveness/effectiveness of legal rules on investment[4]	n.a.	3	4	4	n.a.	2	4	3	n.a.	2	2	3

Source: EBRD *Transition Report,* 1994, 1995, 1996, and 1997.

[1]Most advanced industrial economies would qualify for the 4+ rating for almost all transition indicators.

[2]In 1997, governnance and restructuring.

[3]In 1994, price liberalization and competition policy were grouped together.

[4]In 1997, pledge, bankruptcy, and company laws.

Table 7.3. Classification System for the EBRD Transition Indicators

Transition Element	Category	Description of the Category
Large-scale privatization	1	Little private ownership
	2	Comprehensive scheme almost ready for implementation; some sales completed.
	3	More than 25 percent of large-scale enterprise assets in private hands or in the process of being privatized (with the process having reached a stage at which the state has effectively ceded its ownership rights), but possibly with major unresolved issues regarding corporate governance.
	4	More than 50 percent of state-owned enterprise and farm assets in private ownership.
	4+	Standards and performance typical of advanced industrial economies: more than 75 percent of enterprise assets in private ownership with effective corporate governance.
Small-scale privatization	1	Little progress
	2	Substantial share privatized
	3	Nearly comprehensive program implemented
	4	Complete privatization of small companies with tradable ownership rights
	4+	Standards and performance typical of advanced industrial economies: no state ownership of small enterprises; effective tradability of land.
Enterprise restructuring	1	Soft budget constraints (lax credit and subsidy policies weakening financial discipline at the enterprise level); few other reforms to promote corporate governance.
	2	Moderately tight credit and subsidy policy but weak enforcement of bankruptcy legislation and little action taken to strengthen competition and corporate governance
	3	Significant and sustained actions to harden budget constraints and to promote corporate governance effectively (e.g., through privatization combined with tight credit and subsidy policies and enforcement of bankruptcy legislation).
	4	Substantial improvement in corporate governance, for example, an account of an active corporate control market; significant new investment at the enterprise level.
	4+	Standards and performance typical of advanced industrial economies: effective corporate control exercised through domestic financial institutions and markets, fostering market-driven restructuring.
Price liberalization	1	Most prices formally controlled by the government
	2	Price controls for several important product categories, state procurement at nonmarket prices remains substantial.
	3	Substantial progress on price liberalization: state procurement at nonmarket prices largely phased out.
	4	Comprehensive price liberalization; utility pricing that reflects economic costs.
	4+	Standards and performance typical of advanced industrial economies: comprehensive price liberalization; efficiency-enhancing regulation of utility pricing.
Trade and foreign exchange system	1	Widespread import and export controls or very limited legitimate access to foreign exchange.
	2	Some liberalization of import and/or export controls; almost full current account convertibility in principle but with a foreign exchange regime that is not fully transparent (possibly with multiple exchange rates).
	3	Removal of almost all quantitative and administrative import and export restrictions; almost full current account convertibility.
	4	Removal of all quantitative and administrative import and export restrictions (apart from agriculture) and all significant export tariffs; insignificant direct involvement in exports and imports by ministries and state-owned trading companies; no major nonuniformity of customs duties for nonagricultural goods and services; full current account convertibility.
	4+	Standards and performance norms of advanced industrial economies: removal of most tariff barriers; membership in World Trade Organization (WTO).
Competition policy	1	No competition legislation and institutions.
	2	Competition policy legislation and institutions set up; some reduction of entry restrictions or enforcement action on dominant firms.
	3	Some enforcement actions to reduce abuse of market power and to promote a competitive environment, including break-ups of dominant conglomerates; substantial reduction of entry restrictions.
	4	Significant enforcement actions to reduce abuse of market power and to promote a competitive environment.
	4+	Standards and performance typical of advanced industrial economies: effective enforcement of competition policy; unrestricted entry to most markets.
Banking reform and interest rate liberalization	1	Little progress beyond establishment of a two-tier system.
	2	Significant liberalization of interest rates and credit allocation; limited use of directed credit or interest rate ceilings.

Table 7.3 (*continued*)

Transition Element	Category	Description of the Category
	3	Substantial progress in establishment of bank solvency and of a framework for prudential supervision and regulation; full interest rate liberalization with little preferential access to cheap refinancing; significant lending to private enterprises and significant presence of private banks.
	4	Significant movement of banking laws and regulations toward BIS standards; well-functioning banking competition and effective prudential supervision; significant term lending to private enterprises; substantial financial deepening.
	4+	Standards and performance norms of advanced industrial economies: full convergence of banking laws and regulations with BIS standards; provision of full set of competitive banking services.
Securities markets and nonbank financial institutions	1	Little progress
	2	Formation of securities exchanges, market-makers and brokers; some trading in government paper and/or securities; rudimentary legal and regulatory framework for the issuance and trading of securities.
	3	Substantial issuance of securities by private enterprises; establishment of independent share registries, secure clearance and settlement procedures, and some protection of minority shareholders; emergence of nonbank financial institutions (e.g., investment funds, private insurance and pension funds, leasing companies) and associated regulatory framework.
	4	Securities laws and regulations approaching international standards; substantial market liquidity and capitalization; well-functioning nonbank financial institutions and effective regulation.
	4+	Standards and performance norms of advanced industrial economies: full convergence of securities laws and regulations with international standards; fully developed nonbank intermediation.
Extensiveness of legal rules on investment	1	Legal rules are very limited in scope and impose substantial constraints on creating investment vehicles, security over assets or repatriating profits. Indirect investment is not specifically regulated.
	2	Legal rules are limited in scope and impose significant constraints on creating investment vehicles, adequate security over assets or repatriating profits.
	3	Legal rules do not impose major obstacles to creating investment vehicles, security over assets or repatriating profits. However, they are in need of considerable improvement.
	4	Legal rules do not discriminate between foreign and domestic investors and impose few restrictions on creating a range of investment vehicles and security instruments. Indirect investments is specifically regulated.
	4+	Legal rules closely approximate generally accepted standards internationally and impose few restrictions, including on the creation of sophisticated investment vehicles or security. Indirect investment law is well developed.
Effectiveness of legal rules on investment	1	Legal rules are usually very unclear and often contradictory and the availability of independent legal advice is very limited. The administration of the law is substantially deficient (e.g., little confidence in the abilities and independence of the courts, no or poorly organized security and land registers).
	2	Legal rules are generally unclear and sometimes contradictory. Legal advice is often difficult to obtain. The administration and judicial support of the law is rudimentary.
	3	While legal rules are reasonably clear and ascertainable through legal advice, administration or judicial support of the law is often inadequate (e.g., substantial discretion in the administration of laws, few up-to-date registers).
	4	The law is reasonably clear and legal advice is readily available. Investment laws are reasonably well administered and supported judicially, although that support is sometimes patchy.
	4+	The law is clear and readily ascertainable. Sophisticated legal advice is readily available. Investment law is well supported administratively and judicially, particularly regarding the efficient functioning of courts and the orderly and timely registration of proprietary or security interests.

Source: EBRD *Transition Report*, various issues.

Corporate restructuring is moving along in all three countries, with Latvia and Lithuania again treading in Estonia's footsteps. Through privatization efforts, tight credit policy, cutback in subsidies, and strict enforcement of bankruptcy legislation, Estonia has strived to constrain budgets and promote responsible corporate management. Meanwhile, the other two Baltic countries have pursued more moderate credit and subsidy policies. Further improvements in corporate management and in financial discipline at the enterprise level are still needed throughout the Baltics, preferably accompanied by further actions to break up the dominance of key state-owned firms.

All Baltic countries have made significant gains in price and trade liberalization. Few prices are formally under government control, even though complete price liberalization is yet to be achieved. As discussed in Section II, Estonia is in a unique position regarding trade liberalization with one of the most liberal trade regimes in the region. Latvia and Lithuania have removed most quantitative and administrative import and export restrictions, as well as all significant export tariffs, while average import tariffs on raw materials, intermediate goods, and industrial products are generally moderate.

The significant openness of the trade regimes in the Baltics may in fact prove contentious ahead of the upcoming EU accession negotiations. Remaining tariff barriers in the Baltics may, on the one hand, be lowered even further in connection with the ongoing bilateral negotiations to join the WTO, a prerequisite for EU membership. On the other hand, once a member of the EU, each country will have to raise its external trade tariffs to the common EU level, which is in some cases above the levels currently prevailing in the Baltics. It should also be noted that the Association Agreements between the Baltics and the EU, which entered into force early this year, do not allow the Baltic countries to impose any new tariffs on imports from the EU.

In Estonia, significant enforcement actions have been taken to reduce abuse of market power and promote a competitive environment, including breakups of dominant conglomerates and a substantial reduction in entry restrictions; the country is setting up competition legislation and institutional oversight. Latvia and Lithuania have embarked on similar undertakings, although further efforts are still needed; to reach the level of advanced industrial countries, competition policy and market access will have to be further improved in both countries, in particular in Lithuania.

Banking reform and interest rate liberalization have proceeded at approximately the same pace in all three countries. Interest rates and credit allocation have been liberalized, and progress has been made in the establishment of bank solvency requirements and frameworks for advisory supervision and regulation. Banking sector reforms where more progress is needed include lending to private enterprises and bank privatization. Also, the Baltics still do not provide the full range of competitive banking services available elsewhere in Europe, and further progress is required toward full convergence of banking laws and regulations with the Bank of International Settlement standards.

The development of securities markets and nonbank financial institutions has been rather slow in all three countries. It will be necessary to further develop the legal and regulatory framework to promote the issuance and trading of securities of private enterprises. Furthermore, laws and regulations need to be harmonized with international standards; an independent share register and secure clearing and settlement procedures need to be established; and the rights of minority shareholders need to be protected. Steps should be taken to foster growth and supervision of nonbank financial institutions, such as investment funds, private insurance and pension funds, and leasing companies.

Estonia has also been ahead of the other two Baltic countries regarding investment legislation. Legal rules do not impose major obstacles to the creation of investment opportunities or remittance of profits. The law is reasonably clear in this regard, with legal advice readily available if needed. The judicial and administrative support of the laws are, however, still incomplete. In Latvia and Lithuania, progress has been made to expand and enhance the effectiveness of the legal framework on investment; however, legal rules are not always clear and expert advice can be difficult to obtain. The laws are also less conducive to creating investment vehicles and the judicial and administrative support of the laws need to be further developed. Further efforts should therefore concentrate on bringing the legal framework in line with international standards and on creating a functional court system. In both countries, the governments are committed to these goals, in particular in Lithuania in the context of a significantly intensified privatization campaign.

The French List: Status of the Baltic Countries

As discussed in Section II, a more detailed description of the admission criteria, generally known as the "French list," was proposed during the Copenhagen summit to provide more concrete definitions and guidelines on what is expected of the associated countries. Some of the measures listed in the French list were already included among the EBRD transition indicators, as shown earlier.

Selective economic variables as proposed by the French list are displayed for the Baltic countries for the past four years in Table 7.4. These variables include GDP per capita (in U.S. dollars), meant to capture the general state of development; real GDP growth and foreign direct investment, indicative of potential future progress; inflation; the fiscal balance in terms of GDP, measuring the stance of fiscal policy; the ratio of public debt to GDP; the exchange rate vis-à-vis the U.S. dollar and the deutsche mark, reflecting the stability of monetary policy; and total exports in terms of GDP, gauging the economies' degree of openness.

While the Baltics are still clearly lagging behind as to per capita incomes compared with average industrial country levels (see Table 7.4), the current level of income should be less of a concern ahead of EU membership negotiations. More important will be the EU's assessment of the countries' ability to create wealth fast enough to bring them up to EU standards in a reasonably short time. The Baltics will therefore have to convince the EU that they will exceed the EU average growth rate in the years to come. From Table 7.4 and Table 7.5, which lists some basic economic indicators for the Baltics and the EU for the 1994–96 period, we see that starting in 1996, the three Baltic countries all grew at least as fast as, or even faster than, the estimated EU growth rates. However, real growth rates of 6–11 percent are estimated to be necessary to reach the per capita in-

come level of even the least wealthy EU member states by 2010.[17]

In the years to come, investment and the policies that promote it are key to maintaining rapid growth in transition economies.[18] Given the lack of domestic saving in the Baltics, foreign investment is particularly important. However, foreign direct investment has so far been quite moderate and volatile; while Estonia reached a peak in 1994 with foreign direct investment inflows amounting to 9 percent of GDP, inflows dropped to only 2.5 percent of GDP in 1996.[19] Inflows to Latvia have in recent years amounted to 5–7 percent of GDP. Lithuania has generally been less successful, attracting only about 2 percent of GDP in foreign inflows in 1996 although foreign direct investment is estimated to have reached 4 percent of GDP in 1997. In light of the preceding discussion concerning the high growth rates required to catch up with average EU income levels,

---

[17]See, for example, Federation of Swedish Industries (1996).

[18]See, for example, Fischer, Sahay, and Végh (1996a and 1996b) for a discussion of the growth prospects of transition economies.

[19]The drop in foreign direct investment to Estonia in 1996 can in part be attributed to a decline in investment opportunities in between the completion of sales of small and medium-sized public enterprises and the privatization of larger state enterprises and infrastructure enterprises. However, the decline may also be attributed to a shift in foreign capital inflows to portfolio investments.

Table 7.4. Selected Economic Accession Indicators for the Baltics

Variable	Estonia				Latvia				Lithuania			
	1994	1995	1996	1997	1994	1995	1996	1997	1994	1995	1996	1997
GDP per capita (U.S. dollars)	1,555	2,433	2,959	3,210	1,430	1,880	2,145	2,325	1,131	1,622	2,128	2,575
Real GDP growth (percent)	−1.8	4.3	4.0	10.8	2.1	0.3	3.3	6.5	−9.8	3.3	4.7	5.7
Foreign direct investment, net												
In millions of U.S. dollars	212	202	110	132	155	244	376	415	31	72	152	328
In percent of GDP	9.1	5.6	2.5	2.8	4.2	5.2	7.0	7.2	0.7	1.2	1.9	3.4
Inflation (percent)												
Period average	48	29	23	11	36	25	18	8	72	40	25	9
End of period	42	29	15	3	26	23	13	7	45	36	13	8
General government												
Financial balance (percent of GDP)	2.8	−0.9	−1.5	2.0	−1.7	−2.7	−1.2	1.6	−1.2	−2.6	−2.5	−0.8
Fiscal balance (percent of GDP)	1.3	−1.2	−1.5	2.0	−4.0	−3.3	−1.3	1.3	−4.8	−4.5	−4.6	−1.9
Public debt (percent of GDP)	7.3	6.7	6.9	5.6	14.6	15.3	14.2	11.2	15.3	18.2	23.4	21.2
Local currency (period average) versus												
U.S. dollar	12.99	11.47	12.03	14.10	0.560	0.528	0.551	0.581	4.00	4.00	4.00	4.00
Deutsche mark	8.00	8.00	8.00	8.00	0.345	0.368	0.366	0.335	2.46	2.79	2.66	2.31
Exports in percent of GDP[1]	62	62	53	57	34	36	36	37	47	45	45	45

Sources: IMF, *International Financial Statistics*; national authorities; and IMF staff estimates.
[1]Merchandise exports and net services balance.

and the important role played by FDI in the modernization of transition economies, the Baltics will need to continue to strive to maintain a favorable investment climate, including through the elimination of remaining restrictions to foreign participation in domestic economic activity.

The remaining variables in Table 7.4 show a mixed picture. Despite substantial progress in the past years, the rates of inflation in the Baltics are still significantly above the currently very low EU average; meanwhile, variables measuring the fiscal stance, such as deficit and debt ratios, indicate a notably better position compared with that of the EU (Table 7.5). Furthermore, exchange rates have been stable, reflecting the fixed exchange rate regimes of all three Baltic countries and the degree of openness of their economies. High export growth will also be important to ensure high economic growth, as investments in physical capital primarily will have to come through imported machinery. To capture some of the impact of the prospective member countries' economies on the EU, the ratio of Baltic exports to EU exports is also provided in Table 7.5, clearly highlighting the Baltics' relatively minor impact on EU trade flows.

The remaining indicators included in the French list refer to the convertibility of the local currency and policies on capital movements, the level of social protection, and the existence of a modern fiscal system. All three Baltic countries have liberalized their capital accounts, and they all accepted the obligations of the IMF's Article VIII in mid-1994. More work is needed, however, in the areas of social protection and public sector reform, and further ef-

forts within the Phare Programs will in fact be focused on, inter alia, social sector development and public sector management.

The Maastricht Criteria: Status of the Baltic Countries

The first step toward the EU for the associated member countries of central and eastern Europe is to meet the economic, social, and legal requirements for membership.[20] Among the requirements defined in the Copenhagen Council is the existence of a functioning market economy capable of coping with competitive pressures and market forces within the Union as well as the ability to take on the obligations of membership including the adherence to the aims of EMU. If an associated member country does not meet the Maastricht criteria for EMU participation by the time of EU membership, it will have to adopt the general goals and provisions of the third stage of EMU as a member state with a derogation.[21] This derogation is to be temporary, lasting only until the member state meets the convergence criteria, at which point, according to the EU interpretation,[22] it

---

[20]Other steps toward the EU include decisions on whether to accede to the EU's Social Charter; Latvia recently signed the Social Charter and Estonia is preparing such a step.

[21]See Ilzkovitz (1996) for a good overview of the challenges facing the associated member countries ahead of EMU participation.

[22]Individual countries have at times expressed differing interpretations regarding their obligation to participate in the EMU by the time they meet the Maastricht convergence criteria, suggesting that they could "opt out" of this arrangement.

Table 7.5. Selected Economic Indicators for the Baltics and the EU[1]

Variable	Baltics			European Union		
	1994	1995	1996	1994	1995	1996
Real GDP growth (percent)	−3.7	2.3	4.0	3.0	2.5	1.8
Inflation (average; percent)	52	31	22	3.1	3.1	2.4
Inflation (end of period; percent)	38	29	14	. . .	. . .	2.2
Fiscal balance (percent of GDP)[2]	−2.5	−3.0	−2.5	−5.1	−5.0	. . .
Public debt (percent of GDP)[2]	12.4	13.4	14.7	60.1	64.3	. . .
Memorandum item						
Baltic exports in percent of EU exports[3]				0.25	0.29	0.36

Sources: Eurostatistics; IMF, *International Financial Statistics*; national authorities; and IMF staff estimates.
[1]Referring to the 15 EU member states.
[2]Central government for the EU.
[3]Merchandise exports.

is obliged to participate in the third stage of EMU encompassing the (irrevocable) fixing of parities between the currencies of the qualifying EU member states.[23]

The Maastricht convergence criteria state that to qualify for the EMU, which is to start on January 1, 1999, the following criteria will have to have been met in 1997:

- the rate of *inflation* cannot be more than 1½ percentage points above the average of the three best-performing member states;
- *long-term interest rates* cannot be more than 2 percentage points above the same benchmark;
- the *budget deficit* cannot exceed 3 percent of GDP, unless this ratio has declined "substantially and continuously," or the excess over the reference value is "exceptional and temporary";
- *public debt* cannot exceed 60 percent of GDP, unless the ratio is diminishing "sufficiently" and approaching the reference value at a "satisfactory pace"; and
- the *exchange rate* should have observed the "normal margins" of the Exchange Rate Mechanism (ERM) of the European Monetary System (EMS) for the two preceding years.

From the above list of convergence criteria and from the discussion above, it is clear that the Baltic countries would have little problem today qualifying for the two fiscal criteria; both public debt and fiscal deficits are well below the stipulated levels, in part reflecting the fact that all debt of the former Soviet Union was assigned to Russia by the time of the breakup.[24] Furthermore, the pegged exchange rate regimes chosen by the Baltic countries during their transitions from planned to market economies bode well for their ability to participate in a fixed exchange rate regime centered around the forthcoming "euro."[25]

Meanwhile, more efforts will be needed regarding the other two financial variables. Inflation in the Baltics is still significantly above the EU average, not to say above the rates of inflation of the "best-performing" states.[26] Even more complex is the issue of long-term interest rates. The Baltic countries, just as the other associated member countries in central and eastern Europe, are still in transition to market economies, with highly underdeveloped long-term capital markets; for example, ten-year bond yields, the maturity considered for the convergence criteria, do not yet exist in the Baltic countries. Therefore, the development of financial markets will be a prerequisite for assessing the performance of the Baltics regarding the criterion on interest rate stability. In fact, the absence of developed financial markets in the transitional economies is a symptom of their unreadiness for EMU participation at this stage.

A couple of final caveats may be necessary. First, it should be noted that the Maastricht convergence criteria for EMU participation have to be fulfilled not only by the time a country enters into the third stage but also subsequently on a permanent basis. Therefore, the ability to correct macroeconomic distortions by policies compatible with market economies and EU rules will be as important as the magnitude of the distortions per se. Second, when deciding at which stage to adopt the EMU convergence criteria, the associated member countries should take into account the notion that a premature adoption of excessively tight convergence criteria could slow down the successful completion of necessary structural reforms.

Conclusions

The intention of the Baltics to accede to the EU may have implications for their relations with the IMF. Given the Baltics' explicit desire for closer integration with Europe in general and the EU in particular, a standpoint that probably can be attributed not only to economic arguments but also to geopolitical considerations, it may well be that preparations for accession, such as the approximation of domestic laws to the internal market's *acquis communautaire*, may absorb a large share of already scarce human resources and put strains on domestic administrative capacities. In that context, it is worthwhile noting that, notwithstanding plans to accede to the EU, both Estonia and Latvia have found it advantageous to negotiate programs with the IMF, providing, inter alia, policy advice and precautionary financing. Following the successful expiration in 1997 of its first arrangement under the Extended Fund Facility

---

[23]The derogation of a member state can be abrogated according to a procedure similar to the one employed to decide which member countries will participate in the first round of EMU. This procedure will take place at least every two years, or at the request of the member country with a derogation.

[24]In fact, in the Baltics, to the degree that a gradual increase in public debt would reflect the undertaking of sound investment projects, such a development would not necessarily be unwelcome.

[25]It should be noted that according to the EC Treaty, a two-year formal membership participation in the ERM, without initiating a devaluation, is required to fulfill the exchange rate stability criterion; incidentally, this interpretation is not shared by all current EU member states. In fact, the behavior of the euro is likely to be highly dominated by the current behavior of the deutsche mark, the anchor of the Estonian currency board and one of the five composite currencies constituting the SDR, the anchor of the Latvian fixed exchange rate regime.

[26]Several EU member states currently have rates of inflation below 2 percent.

(EFF), Lithuania at this time does not envisage another program with the Fund. Overall, the measures expected to be undertaken by the Baltics to become members of the EU should be broadly in line with IMF policies, even though there may, at times, be differences of view as regards priorities and the timing of implementation. One such area is trade policy, where the IMF's general advice of lowering tariffs and reducing protection may run counter to EU advice ahead of accession negotiations.

References

Backé, Peter, 1997, "Interlinkages Between European Monetary Union and a Future EU Enlargement to Central and Eastern Europe," *Review of Economies in Transition,* Bank of Finland, Vol. 2, pp. 27–45.

Baltic Review, 1995, *The Baltic States and EU Integration,* Vol. 6 (Winter), pp. 12–13.

Baltic Sea States Summit, 1996, *Presidency Declaration,* Visby, May.

Commission of the European Communities, 1993a, *The Challenge of Enlargement in Commission Opinion on Malta's Application for Membership,* Bulletin, Supplement 4/93 (Brussels).

————, 1993b, *The Challenge of Enlargement in Commission Opinion on the Application by the Republic of Cyprus for Membership,* Bulletin, Supplement 5/93 (Brussels).

————, 1994a, *The Europe Agreements and Beyond: A Strategy to Prepare the Countries of Central and Eastern Europe for Accession,* COM (94) 320 final (Brussels, July).

————, 1994b, *Follow-Up to Commission Communication on "The Europe Agreements and Beyond: A Strategy to Prepare the Countries of Central and Eastern Europe for Accession,"* COM (94) 361 final (Brussels, July).

————, 1995a, *Preparation of the Associated Countries of Central and Eastern Europe for Integration into the Internal Market of the Union,* White Paper, COM(95) 163 final 2 (Brussels, May).

————, 1995b, *Decision of the Council and the Commission on the Conclusion of the Europe Agreements Between the European Communities and Their Member States, of the One Part, and the Republics of Estonia, Latvia, and Lithuania, of the Other Part,* COM(95) 207 final (Brussels, June).

————, 1995c, *Report on the Current State of and Perspectives for Cooperation in the Baltic Sea Region,* COM(95) 609 final (Brussels, November).

————, 1996a, *The Improvement in the External Position of Central and Eastern European Countries,* European Economy, Supplement A, No. 2 (Brussels, February).

————, 1996b, *Reinforcing Political Union and Preparing for Enlargement,* Commission Opinion (Brussels, February).

————, 1996c, *Baltic Sea Region Initiative,* SEC(96) 608 final (Brussels, April).

————, 1996d, *Annotated Summary of Agreements Linking the Communities with Non-Member Countries* (Brussels, June).

————, 1996e, *The Phare Programme Annual Report 1995,* COM (96) 360 final (Brussels, July).

————, 1996f, *Phare—Programme and Contract Information 1996: Estonia, Latvia, Lithuania,* Directorate General External Relations (Brussels).

————, 1996g, *The European Union's Pre-Accession Strategy for the Associated Countries of Central Europe,* Directorate General External Relations (Brussels).

————, 1996h, *Eurostat Yearbook '96—A Statistical Eye on Europe 1985–1995* (Luxembourg).

————, 1997a, *Eurostatistics* (Luxembourg).

————, 1997b, *Agenda 2000—For a Stronger and Wider Union,* Supplement 5/97, COM (97) 200 final (Brussels, July).

European Bank for Reconstruction and Development, 1994, 1995, 1996, 1997, *Transition Reports* (London, October).

Federation of Swedish Industries, 1996, *Nordic Economic Outlook & the Baltics,* No. 2 (July).

Fischer, Stanley, Ratna Sahay, and Carlos A. Végh, 1996a, "Economies in Transition: The Beginnings of Growth," *American Economic Review,* Vol. 86 (May) pp. 229–33.

————,1996b, "Stabilization and Growth in Transition Economies: The Early Experience," IMF Working Paper 96/31 (Washington: International Monetary Fund).

Ilzkovitz, Fabienne, 1996, "Challenges to the Monetary and Exchange Rate Policies of Central and East European Acceding Countries: an EU Perspective," *in Monetary Policy in Central and Eastern Europe: Challenges of EU Integration* (Vienna: Austrian National Bank and the Vienna Institute for Comparative Economic Studies).

International Monetary Fund, 1997, *International Financial Statistics* (Washington).

Pautola, Niina, 1996, "The Baltics and the European Union—On the Road to Membership," *Review of Economies in Transition,* Bank of Finland, Vol. 4, pp 21–40.

Recent Occasional Papers of the International Monetary Fund

173. The Baltic Countries: From Economic Stabilization to EU Accession, by Julian Berengaut, Augusto Lopez-Claros, Françoise Le Gall, Dennis Jones, Richard Stern, Ann-Margret Westin, Effie Psalida, Pietro Garibaldi. 1998.

172. Capital Account Liberalization: Theoretical and Practical Aspects, by a staff team led by Barry Eichengreen and Michael Mussa, with Giovanni Dell'Ariccia, Enrica Detragiache, Gian Maria Milesi-Ferretti, and Andrew Tweedie. 1998.

171. Monetary Policy in Dollarized Economies, by Tomás Baliño, Adam Bennett, and Eduardo Borensztein. 1998.

170. The West African Economic and Monetary Union: Recent Developments and Policy Issues, by a staff team led by Ernesto Hernández-Catá and comprising Christian A. François, Paul Masson, Pascal Bouvier, Patrick Peroz, Dominique Desruelle, and Athanasios Vamvakidis. 1998.

169. Financial Sector Development in Sub-Saharan African Countries, by Hassanali Mehran, Piero Ugolini, Jean Phillipe Briffaux, George Iden, Tonny Lybek, Stephen Swaray, and Peter Hayward. 1998.

168. Exit Strategies: Policy Options for Countries Seeking Greater Exchange Rate Flexibility, by a staff team led by Barry Eichengreen and Paul Masson with Hugh Bredenkamp, Barry Johnston, Javier Hamann, Esteban Jadresic, and Inci Ötker. 1998.

167. Exchange Rate Assessment: Extensions of the Macroeconomic Balance Approach, edited by Peter Isard and Hamid Faruqee. 1998

166. Hedge Funds and Financial Market Dynamics, by a staff team led by Barry Eichengreen and Donald Mathieson with Bankim Chadha, Anne Jansen, Laura Kodres, and Sunil Sharma. 1998.

165. Algeria: Stabilization and Transition to the Market, by Karim Nashashibi, Patricia Alonso-Gamo, Stefania Bazzoni, Alain Féler, Nicole Laframboise, and Sebastian Paris Horvitz. 1998.

164. MULTIMOD Mark III: The Core Dynamic and Steady-State Model, by Douglas Laxton, Peter Isard, Hamid Faruqee, Eswar Prasad, and Bart Turtelboom. 1998.

163. Egypt: Beyond Stabilization, Toward a Dynamic Market Economy, by a staff team led by Howard Handy. 1998.

162. Fiscal Policy Rules, by George Kopits and Steven Symansky. 1998.

161. The Nordic Banking Crises: Pitfalls in Financial Liberalization? by Burkhard Dress and Ceyla Pazarbaşıoğlu. 1998.

160. Fiscal Reform in Low-Income Countries: Experience Under IMF-Supported Programs, by a staff team led by George T. Abed and comprising Liam Ebrill, Sanjeev Gupta, Benedict Clements, Ronald McMorran, Anthony Pellechio, Jerald Schiff, and Marijn Verhoeven. 1998.

159. Hungary: Economic Policies for Sustainable Growth, Carlo Cottarelli, Thomas Krueger, Reza Moghadam, Perry Perone, Edgardo Ruggiero, and Rachel van Elkan. 1998.

158. Transparency in Government Operations, by George Kopits and Jon Craig. 1998.

157. Central Bank Reforms in the Baltics, Russia, and the Other Countries of the Former Soviet Union, by a staff team led by Malcolm Knight and comprising Susana Almuiña, John Dalton, Inci Otker, Ceyla Pazarbaşıoğlu, Arne B. Petersen, Peter Quirk, Nicholas M. Roberts, Gabriel Sensenbrenner, and Jan Willem van der Vossen. 1997.

156. The ESAF at Ten Years: Economic Adjustment and Reform in Low-Income Countries, by the staff of the International Monetary Fund. 1997.

155. Fiscal Policy Issues During the Transition in Russia, by Augusto Lopez-Claros and Sergei V. Alexashenko. 1998.

154. Credibility Without Rules? Monetary Frameworks in the Post–Bretton Woods Era, by Carlo Cottarelli and Curzio Giannini. 1997.

153. Pension Regimes and Saving, by G.A. Mackenzie, Philip Gerson, and Alfredo Cuevas. 1997.

152. Hong Kong, China: Growth, Structural Change, and Economic Stability During the Transition, by John Dodsworth and Dubravko Mihaljek. 1997.

151. Currency Board Arrangements: Issues and Experiences, by a staff team led by Tomás J.T. Baliño and Charles Enoch. 1997.

150. Kuwait: From Reconstruction to Accumulation for Future Generations, by Nigel Andrew Chalk, Mohamed A. El-Erian, Susan J. Fennell, Alexei P. Kireyev, and John F. Wilson. 1997.

149. The Composition of Fiscal Adjustment and Growth: Lessons from Fiscal Reforms in Eight Economies, by G.A. Mackenzie, David W.H. Orsmond, and Philip R. Gerson. 1997.

148. Nigeria: Experience with Structural Adjustment, by Gary Moser, Scott Rogers, and Reinold van Til, with Robin Kibuka and Inutu Lukonga. 1997.

147. Aging Populations and Public Pension Schemes, by Sheetal K. Chand and Albert Jaeger. 1996.

146. Thailand: The Road to Sustained Growth, by Kalpana Kochhar, Louis Dicks-Mireaux, Balazs Horvath, Mauro Mecagni, Erik Offerdal, and Jianping Zhou. 1996.

145. Exchange Rate Movements and Their Impact on Trade and Investment in the APEC Region, by Takatoshi Ito, Peter Isard, Steven Symansky, and Tamim Bayoumi. 1996.

144. National Bank of Poland: The Road to Indirect Instruments, by Piero Ugolini. 1996.

143. Adjustment for Growth: The African Experience, by Michael T. Hadjimichael, Michael Nowak, Robert Sharer, and Amor Tahari. 1996.

142. Quasi-Fiscal Operations of Public Financial Institutions, by G.A. Mackenzie and Peter Stella. 1996.

141. Monetary and Exchange System Reforms in China: An Experiment in Gradualism, by Hassanali Mehran, Marc Quintyn, Tom Nordman, and Bernard Laurens. 1996.

140. Government Reform in New Zealand, by Graham C. Scott. 1996.

139. Reinvigorating Growth in Developing Countries: Lessons from Adjustment Policies in Eight Economies, by David Goldsbrough, Sharmini Coorey, Louis Dicks-Mireaux, Balazs Horvath, Kalpana Kochhar, Mauro Mecagni, Erik Offerdal, and Jianping Zhou. 1996.

138. Aftermath of the CFA Franc Devaluation, by Jean A.P. Clément, with Johannes Mueller, Stéphane Cossé, and Jean Le Dem. 1996.

137. The Lao People's Democratic Republic: Systemic Transformation and Adjustment, edited by Ichiro Otani and Chi Do Pham. 1996.

136. Jordan: Strategy for Adjustment and Growth, edited by Edouard Maciejewski and Ahsan Mansur. 1996.

135. Vietnam: Transition to a Market Economy, by John R. Dodsworth, Erich Spitäller, Michael Braulke, Keon Hyok Lee, Kenneth Miranda, Christian Mulder, Hisanobu Shishido, and Krishna Srinivasan. 1996.

134. India: Economic Reform and Growth, by Ajai Chopra, Charles Collyns, Richard Hemming, and Karen Parker with Woosik Chu and Oliver Fratzscher. 1995.

133. Policy Experiences and Issues in the Baltics, Russia, and Other Countries of the Former Soviet Union, edited by Daniel A. Citrin and Ashok K. Lahiri. 1995.

132. Financial Fragilities in Latin America: The 1980s and 1990s, by Liliana Rojas-Suárez and Steven R. Weisbrod. 1995.

131. Capital Account Convertibility: Review of Experience and Implications for IMF Policies, by staff teams headed by Peter J. Quirk and Owen Evans. 1995.

130. Challenges to the Swedish Welfare State, by Desmond Lachman, Adam Bennett, John H. Green, Robert Hagemann, and Ramana Ramaswamy. 1995.

129. IMF Conditionality: Experience Under Stand-By and Extended Arrangements. Part II: Background Papers. Susan Schadler, Editor, with Adam Bennett, Maria Carkovic, Louis Dicks-Mireaux, Mauro Mecagni, James H.J. Morsink, and Miguel A. Savastano. 1995.

Note: For information on the title and availability of Occasional Papers not listed, please consult the IMF Publications Catalog or contact IMF Publication Services.

173

The Baltic Countries
From Economic Stabilization to
EU Accession

ISBN 1-55775-738-0

MKSAP® 15
Medical Knowledge Self-Assessment Program®

Cardiovascular Medicine

American College of Physicians